FIRSTFRUITS
and
HARVEST

G. H. Lang 1874-1958

FIRSTFRUITS *and* HARVEST

A Study in Resurrection and Rapture

By
G. H. Lang

Kingsley Press
Shoals, Indiana

Firstfruits and Harvest

PUBLISHED BY KINGSLEY PRESS
PO Box 973
Shoals, IN 47581
USA
Tel. (800) 971-7985
www.kingsleypress.com
E-mail: sales@kingsleypress.com

ISBN: 978-1-937428-16-7

Copyright © 1985 by Schoettle Publishing Co., Inc.
Originally published by the author in 1940 and 1946
First Kingsley Press edition 2012

This first Kingsley Press edition is published under license from Schoettle Publishing Co. Inc., Haysville, North Carolina.

All rights reserved. No part of this book may be reproduced or transmitted in any form or by any means, electronic or mechanical, including photocopying, recording or by any information storage and retrieval system without written permission from the publisher, except for the inclusion of brief quotations in a review.

Scripture quotations are usually from the Revised Version.

Printed in the United States of America.

Contents

Introduction 7
1. The Hope 11
2. Who Are Those "of Christ Jesus"? 23
3. The Period of the Parousia 35
4. The Pre-Tribulation Rapture 41
5. An Enquiry as to Man's Constitution and Future, with Remarks on Hades and Paradise 51
6. The Judgment Seat of Christ 73
7. Appendix to Page 26 89

Introduction

"We must not adhere to those systems of doctrine that never can bear an infringement of a view that is held popularly. For instance, perhaps we have all been brought up in the notion that all the children of God, in all ages, compose the church of God. Now it will be found on closer research that this is not supported by the Word of God." (William Kelly, *Occasional Lectures*, vii, 19.)

The world system that occupies the earth is aged and decrepit. Like some vast, worn-out machine it creaks and groans as at the breaking-point. The age is as weary as wicked, and the only solid comfort is that its consummation seems to be nearing. The death-throes of this vast body corporate will be desperate and painful; yet they will be also the birth-throes of a better age.

The chief need of the world is competent government. Even the best disposed and ablest rulers prove signally unequal to relieving the woes of the nations, but for this urgent need the mercy of God has made full provision. He has in readiness a perfect Sovereign for heaven and earth, His own Son, Jesus Christ the Lord, and His coming to earth to assume the government is a chief theme of the Word of God. (Psa. 96:9-14; 97:1: etc.)

In this expectation the apostles of Christ as devout Jews were trained; but their Lord when about to leave them intimated that there were circumstances connected with that expectation which yet awaited disclosure, and that the Spirit of God, Who had visited and inspired the prophets, should come to them also, to abide with them, and to guide them into all the truth, and to disclose unto them those things to come (John 16:13).

One of these yet undisclosed particulars Christ had just hinted in the words of John 14:2-3: "In my Father's house are many abiding places; if it were not so I would have told you; for I go to prepare a place for you. And if I go and prepare a place for you, I come again, and will receive you unto myself; that where I am, there ye may be also."

This intimation was probably as yet obscure to the apostles. It suggested: 1. That for them the Lord had in mind an abode away from the earth in the heavenly regions; 2. That that place was not yet ready, but that He was about to go thither and prepare it for their use; 3. That He would come again from heaven; 4. That at His coming He would take them away from the earth to that prepared region; 5. That this was in order that they might be in His company in His heavenly abode.

Here then is the introduction of the subject of the removal of some of mankind from the earth to dwell in the heavens. In his *Progress of Doctrine in the New Testament* (24), Bernard has well said, and shown, "that there is no part of the later and larger doctrine [of the New Testament] which has not its germs and principles in the words which Christ spake with His own lips in the days of His flesh. It is provided that all which is to be spoken after shall find support and proof from His own pregnant and forecasting sayings." This is a fact, and it is of the first importance for a right interpreting of the New Testament. The four Gospels open the truths expanded in the epistles; the latter must be construed with the former and cannot be rightly explained in separation from them. The doctrine of the rapture is an instance. It is rooted in this germinal saying of our Lord, even as that of the first resurrection is rooted in His words in Luke 20:34-36: "The sons of *this* age marry and are given in marriage: but *they that are accounted worthy to attain* to *that* age [the age to follow this age, the age of the kingdom], and the resurrection which is out from among the dead, neither marry nor are given in marriage: for neither can they die any more [as those individuals raised from the dead before that resurrection had done and could yet do]: for they are equal to angels; and are sons of God, being sons of the resurrection"

The doctrine of the rapture is thus rooted in this germinal saying of our Lord in John 14:2-3. The idea itself was not wholly new. Enoch and Elijah while living had been removed bodily from the earth to the heavenly world; but that a similar honour was open to themselves was probably a new idea to the apostles; nor did Christ here make clear whether the subjects of this favour would be found living at the moment or be raised from the dead. These and other particulars were afterwards revealed by the Spirit, and our present purpose is to set forth briefly some main elements of the New Testament teaching upon this theme.

1
The Hope

1. *The Necessary Change of Body.* Man by constitution is made of and for the earth. He is physically incapable of living in the presence of God (1 Cor. 15:50; 1 Tim. 6:16), so that a change of body is indispensable (1 Cor. 15:50-58; Phil. 3:20-21; 2 Cor. 4:16-5:10). It is not at death but at the coming of the Lord that this change will be effected and we shall be made like Him (Col. 3:4; 1 John 3:1-3).

2. *With the Lord.* The purpose and effect of this removal and change is that the Lord may have us with Himself, like Himself, to share His glory and authority and to assist in ruling His kingdom (John 14:3, 17, 24; 1 Thess. 4:17; Rev. 3:4, 5, 21; 14:4; 17:14; 20:4).

3. *This is Unique in the Ways of God.* The expression "going to heaven" has become a commonplace, used as the equivalent of a sinner being delivered from hell, but it implies vastly more. A king may pardon a rebel liable to death without taking him to live in the royal palace and appointing him to high office and honour. So sinners might have been saved from eternal death and been given eternal life without their ever being removed to the heavens as their abode. This certainly will be the lot of multitudes of the saved and might have been of all. There will be a new earth with saved nations, and God coming down to them, not their being taken up to His region (Rev. 21:1-3, 24). That some of the saved are to be honoured as above indicated seems to be exceptional in the ways of God and is the final secret of His eternal counsels.[1] Since God cannot make any superior to His Son, He can do nothing greater than to cause some to share His Son's glory and authority. This is the highest possible to the creature to all eternity.

---

1. Col. 2:3: omit "even Christ," and read "in which," that is, "the mystery of God in which are all the treasures of wisdom and knowledge hidden." See Alford, and Darby, *New Translation.*

4. *The Principle of Selection.* In view of our sinful state and wicked works it is evident that this "holy calling" to share His own kingdom and glory is given to us by God "not according to our works, but according to His own purpose and grace, which was given us in Christ Jesus before times eternal" (2 Tim. 1:9). But since not all the saved of mankind will enjoy this highest destiny there must be some principle of selection, for God always acts on moral grounds, not arbitrarily or by caprice.

(a) Enoch was translated alive to heaven before that first age developed its worst degree of corruption and long before the judgment of heaven was poured out. Concerning him the Spirit emphasizes that he looked forward to the coming of the Lord and forewarned the wicked of the judgment then to fall (Jude 14:15), as also that he "walked with God" (Gen. 5:24) in such wise that *"before his translation he hath had witness borne to him that he had been well-pleasing unto God"* (Heb. 11:5). Nothing therefore can be clearer than that the unique privilege of translation must be preceded by such a life of faith in God as produces a clear witness, and a holy walk which God already endorses as well-pleasing to Himself, and which He will crown by a removal to His own sphere of the universe. Unless this were the lesson for us of this Christian age why are these pointed comments upon Enoch made in the New Testament?

(b) Concerning certain Old Testament saints we are told that they *desired* that heavenly country, *looked* for that heavenly city, and therefore in practical daily life walked in separation from the world, confessing that they were strangers and pilgrims in the earth. This manner of life amongst the godless and violent was attended by manifold inconveniences and perils (Gen. 13:7-9; 14:22-23; 21:25; 23:4, 16; 26:15-21). The divine comment on these men of faith and this way of living is, "Wherefore God is not ashamed of them, to be called their God: for [that is, it is evident He is not ashamed of them, because] He hath prepared for them a city" (Heb. 11:8-16), which He would not do for any of whom He might be ashamed. This "wherefore" is most significant. It shows that it was this same manner of life, their response and devotion to the call of God's grace, that made sure to them their calling, by God's choice, to the heavenly world. They had not been ashamed to serve the true and living God among men who did not wish to retain Him in their knowledge (Rom. 1:20); He is not ashamed of them who thus confessed Him. They embraced the offer that grace made them of a place in the heavens, and in consequence they walked a sanctified life in separation from the godless; and *therefore* He Who was their sanctifier was not ashamed of them, and shall bring them to glory (Heb. 2:10-11), by the first resurrection.

To us also this applies: to us those of old are set forth as a weighty example (Heb. 11); to us the Scripture, speaking specifically of our obtaining a rich entrance (i.e., by the first resurrection, instead of by the second resurrection after the millennial age) into the eternal kingdom and glory to which we are called, cries: "Give diligence to make your calling and election sure" (2 Pet. 1:10-11; 1 Pet. 5:10). For it was to such as had just confessed Him to be the Christ of God that Jesus solemnly said, "Whosoever shall be ashamed of Me and of My words, of Him shall the Son of Man be ashamed, when He cometh in His own glory, and the glory of the Father, and of the holy angels" (Lk. 9:20-26; comp. Mk. 8:38: Mat. 10:32-33: Lk. 12:8-9; 2 Ti. 2:10-13).

(c) Thus translation, both of the living, as of the dead by the first resurrection, is consequent upon a life of faith which seizes upon the offer of the heavenly calling and shapes its course and conduct accordingly. So the Lord, dealing with the first and select resurrection, spoke of those that are accounted worthy to attain to that age and the resurrection from among the dead (Lk. 20:34-36). "That age" (singular) is not a Bible term for eternity, which is not one age but many, "the ages of the ages" (thirteen times in the Revelation). "That age" is set by Christ in direct contrast to "this age," and so means the age of the kingdom to follow this age. A general resurrection the Jews expected (Jo. 11:34: Acts 24:15), but here Christ speaks of "the resurrection which is out from among the dead" (*tees anastaseōs tees ek nekrōn*). This is the first clear intimation of such a limited, select resurrection (this doctrine also, as has been pointed out, being rooted in a germinal saying of Christ), and its terms are the key to and must control all subsequent instruction upon the subject. And it is made very clear that this resurrection is a privilege to which one must "attain" and be "accounted worthy" thereof. The notion that a share in the first resurrection is a certainty, irrespective of attainment and worthiness, can only be held in direct disregard of this primary declaration by the One who will effect the resurrection and determine who shall participate therein, the Son of God.

It was through Paul that the Holy Spirit saw fit to give in permanent written form fuller particulars as to this theme (1 Cor. 15; 1 Thess. 4), and it is Paul who elsewhere repeats the words of our Lord Jesus just considered, declaring that, whereas justifying righteousness is verily received through faith in Christ, not by our own works, yet, in marked contrast, "the resurrection which is from among the dead (*teen exanastasin teen ek nekrōn*) is a privilege at which one must arrive (*katanteesō*) by a given course of life, even the experimental knowledge of Christ, of the power of His resurrection, and of the fellowship of His sufferings, thereby becoming conformed unto His death (Phil. 3:7-21). Surely the present participle (*summorphizomenos* becoming conformed) is significant, and decisive in favour of the view that it is a process, a course of life that is contemplated.

It has been suggested that Paul here speaks of a present moral resurrection as he does in Romans 6. But in that chapter it is simply a reckoning of faith that is proposed, not a course of personal sufferings. The subject discussed is whether the believer is to continue in slavery to sin (*douleuein*), as in his unregenerate days, or is the mastery (*kurieuō*) of sin to be immediately and wholly broken? It should be remembered that when writing to the Philippians Paul was near the close of his life and service. Could a life so holy and powerful as his be lived without first knowing experimentally the truth taught in Romans 6? Did the Holy Spirit at any time use the apostles to urge others to seek experiences which the writer had not first known, and to which therefore he could be a *witness?* And again, if by the close of that long and wonderful career Paul was still only longing and striving to attain to death to the "old man" and victory over sin, when did he ever attain thereto? Such reflections upon the apostle are unworthy, and, as has been indicated, the experience set forth in Romans 6 is not to be reached, or to be sought, by suffering, by attaining, by laying hold, by pressing on, or any other such effort as is urged upon the Philippians, but by the simple acceptance by faith of what God says He did for us in Christ in relation to the "old man."

Thus this suggested exposition is neither sound experimental theology nor fair exegesis. Paul indicates as plainly as language can do that the first resurrection may be missed. His words are: "*If by any means* I *may* arrive at the resurrection which is out from among the dead." "If by any means" (*ei pōs*) "I may" – "if" with the subjunctive of the verb—cannot but declare a condition; and so on this particle in this place Alford says, "It is used when an end is proposed, but failure is presumed to be possible": and so Lightfoot: "The apostle states not a positive assurance, but a modest hope": and Grimm-Thayer (Lexicon) give its meaning as, "If in any way, if by any means, if possible," and Ellicott to the same effect says, "the idea of an attempt is conveyed, which may or may not be successful." Both Alford and Lightfoot regard the passage as dealing with the resurrection of the godly from death, and Ellicott's note is worth giving in full. "'The resurrection from the dead'; i.e., as the context suggests, the *first* resurrection (Rev. 20:5), when, at the Lord's coming the dead in Him shall rise first (1 Thess. 4:16), and the quick be caught up to meet Him in the clouds (1 Thess. 4:17); comp. Luke 20:35. The first resurrection will include only true believers, and will apparently precede the second, that of non-believers, and disbelievers, in point of time. Any reference here to a merely ethical resurrection (Cocceius) is wholly out of the question." With the addition that the second resurrection will include believers not accounted worthy of the first, this note is excellent.

The sense and force of the phrase "if by any means I may arrive" are surely fixed beyond controversy by the use of the same words in Acts 27:12: "the more part advised to put to sea from thence, *if by any means* they could *reach* [arrive at] Phoenix, and winter there" (*ei pōs dunainto katanteesantes*), which goal they did *not* reach.

Further, speaking upon the very subject of the resurrection and the kingdom promised afore by God, Paul used the same verb, again preceded by conditional terms, saying (Acts 26:6-8), "unto which promise our twelve tribes, earnestly serving God night and day, hope to *attain.*" Here the force of *elpizei katanteesai* "unto which they hope to attain" is the same as his words in Philipplans *ei pōs kantanteeso,* "if by any means I may attain." This hope of the Israelite of sharing in Messiah's kingdom is plainly conditional (Dan. 12:2-3). It is assured to such an Israelite indeed as Daniel (12:13), and to such a faithful servant of God in a period of great difficulty as Zerubbabel (Hag. 2:23). It was also offered to Joshua the high priest, but upon conditions of obedience and conduct. Joshua had been relieved of his filthy garments and arrayed in noble attire (Zech. 3:1-5), but immediately his symbolic justification before Jehovah had been thus completed, and his standing in the presence of God assured, the divine message to him is couched in conditional language: "And the Angel of Jehovah protested unto Joshua, saying, Thus saith Jehovah of hosts, If thou wilt walk in My ways, and if thou wilt keep My charge, then thou also shalt judge My house, and shalt also keep My courts, and I will give thee places to walk among these that stand by" (ver. 6, 7).

It is at this point that the "ifs" of the Word of God come in, and are so solemn and significant. Whenever the matter is that of the pardon of sin, the justifying of the guilty, the gift of eternal life, Scripture ever speaks positively and unconditionally. The sinner is "justified freely by God's grace," and "the free gift of God is eternal life" (Rom. 3:24; 6:23), in which places the word "free" means free of conditions, not only of payment. Eternal life therefore is what is called in law an absolute gift, in contrast to a conditional gift. The latter may be forfeited if the condition be not fulfilled; the former is irrevocable. But as soon as the sinner has by faith entered into this standing before God, then the Word begins at once to speak to him with "ifs." From this point and forward every privilege is conditional.

It is truly "in all wisdom and prudence" that God has made known to us the mystery of His will (Eph. 1:8-9). The indispensable minimum, justification, without which no further blessing is possible, and which the sinner is utterly unable to acquire, having no nature that can produce ought acceptable to God, this God grants freely through the atoning work of the Lord Jesus. But now that a new nature has been implanted by grace, capable through the Spirit of pleasing God, all attainment is made conditional upon the exertion that this new nature is able to make, and must make. The whole promised land, together with the title to share it and the power to conquer it, are gifts of covenant grace, but no one shall get an inch more than he sets his own foot upon, by the use of the power freely granted to faith that obeys. And some who had equal title with the rest shall not reach the inheritance at all, though neither shall they ever get back to Egypt. "Let him that readeth understand," and ponder the "ifs" of the epistle to the Hebrews.[2]

The comments of Mr. David Baron upon the incident of Joshua are impressive (*The Visions and Prophecies of Zechariah*, 103-105). I extract the following. "The word 'protested' means *solemnly* to protest, and is intended to express the solemnity and importance of the charge about to be made. The expressions, 'Walk in My ways' and 'Keep My charge' are frequently used in the Pentateuch for 'holding on in the way of life, well-pleasing to God, and for keeping the charge given by God.' The first part of the charge refers particularly to Joshua's personal attitude towards the Lord—to fidelity in his personal relations to God; and the second to the faithful performance of his *official* duties as high priest. And the reward of his thus studying (in his personal and official capacity) to present himself approved unto God will be (a) 'Then thou shalt also judge My house . . .' (b) 'And shalt also keep My courts . . .' (c) But the climax of promise in this verse is reached in the last clause, 'And I will give thee places to walk among these that stand by. . .'

"'These that stand by'—as we see by comparing the expression with verse 4—are the angels, who were in attendance on the Angel of Jehovah, and who 'stood before Him' ready to carry out His behests. The Jewish Targum. . . is, I believe, nearer the truth [than many Christian commentators] when it paraphrases the words, 'In the resurrection of the dead I will revive thee, and give thee feet walking among these seraphim.' Thus applied to the future the sense of the whole verse would be this: 'If thou wilt walk in My ways and keep My charge, thou shalt not only have the honour of judging My house and keeping My courts, but when thy work on earth is done thou shalt be transplanted to higher service in heaven, and "have

---

2. See my *Firstborn Sons.*

places to walk" among these pure, angelic beings who stand by Me, hearkening unto the voice of My word' (Psa. 103:20-21). Note the 'ifs' in this verse, my dear reader, and lay to heart the fact that, while pardon and justification are the free gifts of God to all that are of faith, having their source wholly in His infinite and sovereign grace, and quite apart from work or merit on the part of man, the honour and privilege of acceptable service and future reward are conditional upon our obedience and faithfulness: therefore seek by His grace and in the power of His Spirit to 'walk in His ways and to keep His charge,' and in *all things,* even if thine be the lot of a 'porter' or 'doorkeeper' in the House of God, to present thyself approved unto Him, in remembrance of the day when 'we must all be made manifest before the judgment-seat of Christ, that each one may receive the things done in the body, according to what he hath done, whether it be good or bad' (2 Cor. 5:10)."

By virtue of their relationship to Abraham all Israelites are natural sons of the kingdom which is the goal of their national hopes according to the purpose and promise of the God of Abraham; but the King has told them plainly, first, that Abraham, Isaac and Jacob, together with all the prophets—that is, all the men of faith and devotion—shall be in that kingdom, but secondly, that it is very possible that some of the sons of the kingdom may forfeit their entrance thereinto (Matt. 8:10-12: Luke 13:28-29); for there are those who may have been first in privilege and opportunity who shall be last in final attainment.

If, therefore, an Israelite attains to that kingdom it will be on the basis of a covenant made by God with his federal head, Abraham; the source of which covenant is the grace of God in Christ, the working principle of which on man's side is faith proving itself by obedience. Wherein now does this differ in basic principle from that new and better covenant which introduces to better, that is, to heavenly privileges, to sharing the heavenly sphere of that same kingdom, not only its earthward side? This new and higher order of things is also derived from a covenant made with our federal Head, its source is in that same grace of God, its working principle on our side is a faith that proves its quality in obedience.

Moreover, since the man of true faith in that earlier age could aspire to this same heavenly city and country as ourselves there manifestly was no difference in his position and ours in this matter, though it may be he had only a more distant view and not so full a revelation of the purpose of God in all this project. So that if they of old could miss their share, on what principle of righteousness shall we be exempted from their need of diligence and obedience? Such exemption not only would contain an invidious and inexplicable distinction, but it would prove highly dangerous to our moral fibre and our zeal for godliness. And has not this been seen? We heard it boldly stated from a platform, that the sharing in the bridal glories of the wife of the Lamb is guaranteed absolutely no matter what our practical life may or may not have been. But obviously if the very highest of all honours cannot possibly be forfeited plainly *nothing* is forfeitable, and the whole notion of reward for effort, so heavily emphasized in Holy Scripture, is swept away. For ourselves we repudiate this common teaching as grossly immoral in its tendency, the sheerest antinomianism, and flatly repugnant to the Word.

The Lord told His disciples that status in the kingdom of the heavens was to be determined by the measure of obedience and of having encouraged others to obedience, and He as clearly added that entrance itself into that kingdom was conditional upon a certain degree of practical righteousness (Matt. 5:19-20). He further plainly warned the apostles themselves that except they turned from their high-mindedness, and became as humble as a little child, they should on no account enter into the kingdom (Matt. 18:3). And this same possibility of missing our inheritance by practical misconduct became a stock element in the apostolic teaching of their converts, and most especially and notably of Paul (1 Cor. 6:7-10; Gal. 5:19-21; Eph. 5:5).

It followed that godly Israelites, bent on securing a share with Abraham in the kingdom of Messiah, served God, as Paul says, with the utmost earnestness and ceaselessly: "earnestly (*en ekteneia*) serving God night and day" (Acts 26:7). It is an intensive form of this very word which Paul employs in the Philippian passage (*epekteinomenos*) to describe his own strenuous endeavours in godly service and suffering to reach that same goal, the out-resurrection. The word pictures the racer leaning far forward, stretched out toward the goal, straining every fibre to win the coveted prize. It is the sharpest possible rebuke to the complaisant idea that so great a reward is guaranteed to all believers irrespective of piety, zeal, devotion, and life-long perseverance.

Nor is there warrant for the assertion that to Paul only or even first were these themes made known. He indeed learned them direct from the Lord, but so did other "holy apostles and prophets," according to his own statement (Eph.3:5). These mighty truths were as much the need of and as much the property of those many saints whom Paul never taught as of that portion of the church of God to whom he ministered. And that the other apostles did in fact know and teach the truth of a select resurrection, prior to the general resurrection of all men, and thus knew and taught prior even to Paul's conversion, is seen from the statement in Acts 4:2, that from the very earliest days they "proclaimed in Jesus the resurrection which is out from among the dead" (*teen anastasin teen ek nekrōn*). The clearness of their understanding of this first, select resurrection, of which the Lord had spoken while with them, is shown by the definiteness and vigour with which they announced it, for *katangellō*, in the A.V. weakly rendered "preach," means "to proclaim with authority, as commissioned to spread the tidings *throughout* those who hear them" (Westcott, on 1 John 1:5). Therefore such a resurrection was not revealed for the first time when Paul wrote to the Thessalonians; those who were apostles before him made it their business to announce this truth to all to whom they proclaimed the gospel, for, as Paul himself tells us, it was the "commandment of the eternal God" that the secret counsel of which the first resurrection is part should be "made known unto all the nations" (Rom. 16:26), which demanded that other heralds before and besides Paul should receive and proclaim the message.

When first writing to the Thessalonians he could say that they already "knew perfectly" about the day of the Lord, and when writing again he added that he had told them about these things when with them (1 Thes. 5:2; 2 Thes. 2:5). This is further shown by the way he speaks without explanation of those who "will be left unto the presence of the Lord," to His parousia. How could he have enlarged when with them upon these topics and yet not even himself have known about the vital matter of the first resurrection? Yet this is necessarily involved in the assertion that this truth was not made known before the first letter to the Thessalonians.

2
Who Are Those "of Christ Jesus"?

But it is urged that two important scriptures upon the topic of resurrection seem to contemplate all believers as sharing in the first resurrection. These are 1 Thess. 4 and 1 Cor. 15.

The former passage speaks of those who "have fallen asleep through Jesus" (1 Thess. 4:14, R.V. marg.). Is this of necessity the fact concerning the end of all believers? Is there not such a thing as death *through Satan,* acting as the executioner of the sentence of the court of heaven against a believer's sins? (1 Cor. 5:5; 11:30; Acts 5:10: comp. 1 Tim. 1:19-20; 1 Jo. 5:16-17; Jas. 5:19-20).

Man through sin is by nature in the power of Satan as the one who, by his angel servants, ends human life when the Most High requires.[1] But the sinner who in faith submits to Christ is transferred from Satan's authority and is put under that of the Son of God (Col. 1:13), and thenceforth the Evil One cannot touch him (1 Jo. 5:18). In life his Lord protects him and in death puts him to sleep. But on account of gross sin, of living again as if a servant of Satan, he may be "delivered unto Satan," as regards his present experience (Matt. 5:23, 26; 6:13; 18:34-35) and his bodily life, in which case Satan may be permitted to cut short his life, as the above cited passages show.

It is not such a death that is "gain" within the meaning of Phil. 1:21. When Paul wrote of death as "gain" he made no general statement concerning all believers. He said, "For *to me* to live is Christ and to die is gain." At that time he was a prisoner, and it was not certain that he would not shortly die for the faith. That was the death immediately in question, and similarly such an one as the faithful Stephen, dying as a witness for Christ, could say, "Lord Jesus, receive my spirit." The Lord accepted the trust, and the simple record of that dreadful moment is, "he slept." Doubtless not martyrs alone but each who can truly say, "for to me to live is Christ" may add truly, "to die is

---
1. Heb. 2:14; Acts 12:23; Luke 12:20, marg. "they," i.e., angels: contrast Job 2:6.

gain." Those who thus fall asleep will, as we expect, share in the first resurrection; others have no guarantee that they will do so.

But it is further urged that in 1 Cor. 15:51, the Scripture declares that though "we shall not all sleep," but some be alive at the descent of the Lord, yet "we shall *all* be changed," and surely, says the objector with emphasis, *all* means *all*. Truly; but in verse 22, "For as in Adam all die, so also in the Christ shall all be made alive,'" "all" means all of mankind, for every child of Adam will at some time be raised by Christ (Jo. 5:28, 29). But not all at the first resurrection (Rev. 20:5). Therefore in this very chapter "all" means different things, and in verse 51 requires limiting, since it refers to a smaller company than in verse 22.

The last and immediate context is in verses 48-49, which speak of those who are to "bear the image of the heavenly," that is, are to share with the Lord in His heavenly form, glory, and sovereignty. Now the more difficult, and therefore the more probable reading here is as in the R.V. margin: "As we have borne the image of the earthy, *let us* also bear the image of the heavenly." It is evident that one copying a document is not likely to insert by mistake a more difficult word or idea than is in the manuscript before him; so that, as a general rule, the more difficult reading is likely to have been the original reading. Moreover, in this case "let us also bear" is so well attested by the manuscripts as to have been adopted as the true reading by Lachmann, Tischendorf, Tregelles, Alford, and Westcott and Hort, and is given as the text in the latest editions of the Greek Testament, those of Nestle and Von Soden. Ellicott prefers the common reading, but on subjective and internal grounds only, and his remark on the external authority is emphatic: "It is impossible to deny that the subjunctive, *phorēsōmen* is supported by very greatly preponderating authority." Alford (on Romans 9:5) well says, "that no conjecture [i.e., as to the true Greek text] arising from doctrinal difficulty is ever to be admitted in the face of the consensus of MSS and versions." Weymouth gives the force well by the rendering "*let us see to it* that we also bear."

By this exhortation the apostle places upon Christians some responsibility to see that they secure that image of the heavenly which is indispensable to inheriting "the kingdom of God" (ver. 50). In this Paul is supported by Peter, who also writes of that "inheritance which is reserved in heaven" (1 Pet. 1:4), which he describes by the later statement that "the God of all grace called you unto *His eternal glory* in Christ" (5:10). But Peter goes on to urge the called to "give the more diligence to make your calling and election sure" (2 Pet. 1:10), thus showing that this calling to share the glory of God has to be made sure. He is not at all discussing justification by faith or suggesting that it must be made sure by works done after conversion. Justification and eternal life are not in the least his subject. He writes expressly to those "who have [already] obtained like precious faith with us in the righteousness of our God and Saviour Jesus Christ" (2 Pet. 1:1). The calling of grace is to share in God's own eternal glory, or, as Paul expresses it, to share God's "own kingdom and glory," and he tells us that he exhorted, encouraged, yea, and testified, to the end that his children in faith should "walk worthily of God" Who had called them to such supreme dignity (1 Thess. 2:11-12).

Since therefore this most honourable calling must be "made sure" by "walking worthily," in order that we may be "counted worthy of the kingdom of God, for which ye also suffer" (2 Thess. 1:5), the reading "let us also bear the image of the heavenly" becomes consistent and important. Thus 1 Cor. 15:51-52 is addressed to those who are assumed (whether it be so or not) to have responded to that exhortation, and it will mean that "we [who shall be accounted worthy to bear that heavenly image] shall not all sleep, but we shall all be changed." Of that company it is strictly true that *all* means *all*.

Further, the primary antecedent to verse 52 is in verse 23: "But each [shall be made alive] in his own order: Christ the firstfruits; then they that are Christ's in His Parousia: then the end. . . ." Does not the whole sentence, in the light of other passages, carry the force: But each shall be made alive, not all at the same hour, but each in his own class or company (*tagma*); firstfruit, Messiah; then, next, those of the Messiah, i.e., in His character as firstfruit, at His Parousia; then, later, the end of all dispensations, involving the resurrection of all, saved and unsaved, not before raised? Here is additional reason for R. C. Chapman's view (to be considered later) that the first resurrection is one of "firstfruits," and not of all who will be finally raised in the "harvest" of eternal life.

The translation "they that are Christ's" is not an exact rendering. The Greek reads: "then those *of the Christ* (*hoi tou Christou*) in His Parousia," and it is not a question of what these words may mean to an English reader today with his mind obsessed by a certain theory, but what did they convey to a Greek ear of the day when they were written (see Appendix).

In the ideal and possibility all who are "in Christ" are "of Christ," but that it is possible to be a believer on Him unto salvation from hell and not to be of that privileged personal circle which He will acknowledge before God, angels, and men as His companions, is plainly taught in the Word. "If I wash thee not, thou [Peter, my believing, devoted follower until now] hast no part *with Me*"—not "*in* Me," that would have forfeited *all*, including salvation; but "*with Me*," which means that unwashed thou canst not continue in My company, My circle (John 13:8). Again, "Thou hast a few names in Sardis who did not defile their garments, and they shall walk [walk about habitually, *peripateesousin*] *with Me* in white, for they are worthy"; that is, they shall be My companions (Rev. 3:4: compare the personal associates of king Rehoboam, those that had "grown up with him," (1 Kin. 12:7-10). With these who have thus walked with Christ in humiliation and shall walk with Him in glory contrast those mentioned in John 6:66: "Upon this many of His disciples went back, and walked no more with Him." But of those who go on with Him He graciously adds, "The one overcoming shall *thus* [as the consequence and counterpart of having walked in white on earth, of having 'kept himself unspotted from the world,' Jas. 1:27]— shall *thus* be arrayed in white raiment [as a companion of the King; indeed, as His wife, Rev. 19:8]; and I will in no wise blot his name out of the book of life, and I will confess his name before My Father and before His angels"; the King's public acknowledgment that such are of His honoured and intimate circle.[2]

---

2. Rev. 3:4, 5: comp. Luke 12:9, with the use the apostle and the early church made of that saying, as in 2 Tim. 2:11-13.

Who Are Those "of Christ Jesus"?

The fact that such as show special trust in and fidelity to God are granted intimacy with Him beyond others is very natural and it runs throughout Scripture. Instances are: Abraham, peculiarly the friend of God, from whom Jehovah would hide none of His purposes (Gen. 18:17-19): Moses, privileged beyond others of the people of God with mouth to mouth converse with Him, because he was faithful (Num. 12:7-8): the prophets, without informing whom Jehovah would not act (Amos 3:7): of which Elisha is a notable instance, as witness the tone of surprise in his words, *"Jehovah hath hid it from me and hath not told me!"* (2 Kin. 4:27). So God, reproving false prophets, says: "Who [of them] hath stood in the council of Jehovah?" and, "If they had stood in My council" (Jer. 23:18, 22)—not counsel, as A.V., but in "My secret council," as the Hebrew means, whither faithful prophets were transported in spirit (1 Kin. 22:19).

Thus also in the New Testament we learn of very many hundreds who believed on Jesus when He was here (1 Cor. 15:6, e.g.), but of these, some few enjoyed His special love, as the Bethany family (John 11:5); a small band were honoured to share peculiarly His toil, ministry, reproach, *and company,* and will therefore be specially honoured in His kingdom (Lk. 22:28-30; Rev. 22:14): of which few again a smaller circle were more especially favoured with His confidence (Lk. 9:28; Matt. 26:37), and one was loved above them all (Jo. 13:23; 19:26, 21:7, 20).

But as there is no respect of persons, no favouritism, with the Lord, as we are repeatedly and emphatically assured (Col. 3:25; 1 Pet. 1:17: etc.), there must have been reason for this distinguishing of some. In John 15:14-15, Christ lays down its condition in the words: "No longer do I call you slaves [though it is to be well noted from the openings of the epistles that that is exactly what they continued evermore to call themselves]; for the slave knoweth not what his lord doeth: but I have called you friends; for all things that I heard from My Father I have made known unto you." Thus as with Abraham His friend, so with these, He had hid nothing from them, had had no secrets, but had made known unto them all that He had heard. But the terms of this incomparable friendship were, and are, "Ye are My friends if ye do the things which I command you," a condition nowhere attached to the forgiveness of sins or to the obtaining of eternal life, but of the simple nature of things in *friendship* between the Creator and the creature, the King and the subject. To this privileged circle all indeed may attain, but it is reached by such only as pay the (in reality) purely nominal but quite unavoidable price of full obedience to their Saviour as their *Lord*.

Thus also in Hebrews 3:12-14, we learn that "we have become companions[3] of the Messiah (*metochoi tou Christou*), if it be so that (*eanper*) we hold fast the beginning of our confidence firm unto the end." And in verse six preceding we are told that we are the household over which the Son of God is ruler "if we hold fast our boldness and the glorying of our hope firm unto the end." Israel, though redeemed by blood and delivered, did not become the "house" of God until one whole year after redemption (Ex. 40:1); and, though the people of God by covenant and redemption, they only narrowly escaped the penalty of never having God dwelling among them and so of not being to Him as a house (Ex. 33:1-3). To be a pardoned rebel, restored to being a loyal subject of the sovereign, is one thing, and is great indeed, but to be a member of the royal house, a chosen intimate of the sovereign, is much greater. His pardon of the rebel, sealed and delivered, God *never* recalls; but the privilege of belonging to His Son's personal circle is contingent and may be forfeited.

The type of tabernacle and temple when taken in its entirety shows that the "house" of God may be forsaken by Him and be temporarily destroyed (Jer. 7:12; Psa. 78:60-61; Jer. 12:7; Psa. 74:7; Matt. 23:38); and the New Testament solemnly declares the same as to the believer: "Know ye not that ye are a sanctuary of God, and the Spirit of God dwelleth in you. If any man destroyeth the sanctuary of God [mars it—see Jer. 17:7, 9, where the LXX use this word—so rendering the house unfit as a dwelling for the Holy One], him shall God destroy (see 1 Cor. 5:5: etc.), for the sanctuary of God is holy, which sanctuary ye are" (1 Cor. 3:16-17). The believer who so lacks the spirit of Christ, and so walks according to flesh, as to incur that

---

3. Darby, New Translation, note: "I use the word 'companions' as being the same one as in c.1:9 metochoi, to which, I doubt not, it alludes; that is, to the passage quoted, Ps. 45. 'Partakers of Christ' has indeed quite a different sense."

judgment, will indeed, by the changeless grace of God and through the eternal virtue of redemption by the precious blood of Christ, be himself, as to his person, saved, yet only "so as through fire" (ver. 15); but such will not be sharers of the privileges pictured as being the "house" of God or "companions of the Messiah," the King. But inasmuch as all who rise in the first resurrection *will* share those very privileges (Rev. 20:4-6), it results that such as are adjudged by the Lord unworthy thereof will not have part in that resurrection, even as the many scriptures reviewed declare.

Thus the expressions "fallen asleep through Jesus" and "those of Him in His Parousia" (those who are to be companions with Him during the period of His "presence" as King of this earth), both allow for the solemn possibility of some who might have been "accounted worthy to attain unto that age [of the Presence] and the resurrection which is from among the dead" (Lk. 20:35) failing to attain thereto.

Passages which deal with a matter from the point of view of God's plan and willingness use general, wide terms to cover and to disclose His whole provision. But these must be ever considered in connection with any other statements upon the same subject which reveal what God foresees of the human element which, by His own creation of responsible creatures, He permits to interact with His working. Out of these elements, through self-will in the believer, arises the possibility of individuals not reaching unto the whole of what the grace of God had offered in Christ.

The isolation of the former class of passages produced Calvinism, of the latter Arminianism. Truth is found by construing all Scripture together. The principle of the divine provision is *grace:* the principle of our attaining is *faith;* and "according to your faith be it unto you" is the inflexible condition. Now faith is not merely an apprehending of ideas by the intellect, nor only the assent of the reason, though it includes of necessity both of these elements: faith is a principle of action which produces obedience to God and works out in love to men. Incipient faith obeys God upon the primary point of trusting to Christ for salvation from wrath, and it secures that primary benefit for which it trusts. Developing faith obeys God upon various successive points of His holy will; this issues in sanctity of character and purity of conduct; and according to this advance of faith in practical godliness will be the weight of glory which each will be capable of bearing. Any particular possibility for which one's measure of faith does not qualify will not be obtained. "The path of sorrow is not indeed the meriting, but the capacitating preparation for glory" (Moule on Rom. 8:18).

It is unquestionable that this unchanging, because unavoidable, rule operates undeviatingly as to benefits available in this life: the Scripture shows plainly that it operates as to benefits available beyond this life. Of these one is the sharing in the first resurrection and so inheriting the kingdom of God. There is not any ground in Scripture or reason why these particular privileges should be an exception to the invariable rule stated; for the rule lies in the essential nature of man and his relationships with God, and no suspension or exception seems possible so long as God is God and man is man. Apart from faith it is impossible for man to be pleasing to God or for God to grant to him the blessing of such as please Him. The measure of blessing *in the possibility* is the immeasurable merit of Christ, freely made available to sinners by the grace of God: the measure of blessing *in actual attainment* is our faith, faith as above defined and evidenced. Therefore both translation and the better resurrection are consequent upon a life of faith that pleases God (Heb. 11:5, 35).

> Such faith in us, O God, implant,
> And to our prayers Thy favour grant,
> Through Jesus Christ, Thine only Son,
> Who is our fount of health alone.

When it is said that the acceptance of the believer in Christ involves the imputation to him of all the acceptability of Christ, and that he is thereby qualified to share the eternal glory of Christ in the presence of the Father, and that consequently his own life and works can have no place in the matter, we point out that, inasmuch as the merit of Christ is imputed judicially to every believer equally, therefore every believer should of necessity share equally in all and

Who Are Those "of Christ Jesus"?

every privilege, and no distinction in reward would be possible, one star could not then differ from another star in glory. But the opposite of this is taught in the Word. The imputation of righteousness in Christ gives to every believer equality of standing and of opportunity, but it does not, and cannot, do away with the necessity for faith, or alter the rule that attainment is according to faith.

It being therefore the case that the first resurrection, while open indeed to all, is a prize which must be attained, and which, like every prize, may be forfeited, it is at once made clear why in Rev. 20:4-6, where the two resurrections are set, one at the opening of the Millennial kingdom and the other at its close, it is said that "blessed and holy" is he that hath part in the former, including pre-eminently those who in varying degree had suffered for and with Jesus and for the word of God. And that some believers not accounted worthy of that resurrection, will rise in the second resurrection unto eternal life, though they will have missed reigning with Christ in His Kingdom, fitly explains why at the final judgment the book of life will be opened and searched (Rev. 20:11-15). Were it known as a fact that no possessors of eternal life would or could be there this examining of the book of life would not be required, nor should we expect the statement that "if any was not found written in the book" he was cast into the lake of fire; for in that event the natural expression would be "as their names were not found, etc."

A correct understanding of future events is of high value in the life of the Christian, but it is not fundamental to the gospel, neither does any rearranging of the order or particulars of those events imperil the faith. Men of undoubted orthodoxy and greatly used of God have taken very divergent views on these topics, which teaches that great names cannot prove any one view to be the true meaning of Scripture. On the other hand, this divergence should assure toleration and earnest research, so that more light may be gained and ever closer agreement be reached.

It is worthy of mention that Hudson Taylor and R. C. Chapman held the view here advocated. In the Appendix to his small work on The Song of Songs, entitled *Union and Communion* (ed. 5, p. 83),

Hudson Taylor wrote of such as "if saved, are only half-saved:[4] who are for the present more concerned about the things of this world than the things of God. To advance their own interests, to secure their own comfort, concerns them more than to be in all things pleasing to the Lord. They *may* form part of that great company spoken of in Rev. 7:9-17, who come out of the great tribulation, but they will not form part of the 144,000, 'the first-fruits unto God and to the Lamb' (Rev. 14:1-5). They have forgotten the warning of our Lord in Luke 21:34-36; and hence they are not 'accounted worthy to escape all these things that shall come to pass, and to stand before the Son of Man.' They have not, with Paul, counted 'all things but loss for the excellency of the knowledge of Christ Jesus the Lord,' and hence they do not 'attain unto' *that* resurrection from among the dead, which Paul felt he might miss, but aimed to attain unto.

"We wish to place on record our solemn conviction that not all who are Christians, or think themselves to be such, will attain to that resurrection of which St. Paul speaks in Phil. 3:11, or will thus meet the Lord in the air. Unto those who by lives of consecration manifest that they are not of the world, but are looking for Him, 'He will appear without sin unto salvation'."

Robert Chapman about the year 1896 issued a series of *Suggestive Questions*. Number 10 includes the following: "Are not the redeemed in Rev. 4 and 5 the same with those in ch. 20:4, 'Thrones and they sat upon them'? (verse 5) 'This is the first resurrection.' Is it not a resurrection of firstfruits?" ... Now in the essential nature of the case firstfruits are but a portion of the whole harvest, and so the Question proceeds: 'And the rest of the dead (in the same verse) do they not include all the family of God? not the wicked dead only. Hence, in verse 12, 'Another book was opened, which is the book of life: and the dead were judged out of those things which were written in the books, according to their works' (verse 15). 'And

---

4. We do not understand this expression to imply doubt as to the completeness of the believer's standing in Christ as justified; in this respect he is "kept safe from wrath" (Rom. 5:9). But the practical outworking of salvation in this life admits of degrees. There was brought to a keen-witted Christian I knew one who was said to have been "saved." The other had at once detected the smell of tobacco and enquired: "How much of him is saved?"

whosoever was not found written in the book of life was cast into the lake of fire'."

Further as to this last passage, the exact rendering in the Revised Version, "*if* any was *not* found written in the book of life he was cast into the lake of fire," by its negative form strongly supports this view. If it should be said of the crowd at a platform barrier that, *If* any was found *not* to have a ticket he was refused admittance, no one would suggest the meaning that *not one* of all who were there had a ticket or was allowed to pass.

The late Mr. E. S. Pearce was intimately acquainted with Mr. Chapman's views for he lived with him many years. He wrote to me as follows: "It was Mr. Chapman's desire that, by so walking with God and by obedience to His Word in *all things,* he might not shut himself out from the honour of reigning with Christ. He saw no authority from the Scripture for saying that all the children of God would. Rev. 20:4, 'And they sat upon them,' Mr. Chapman considered were distinguished persons, not *all* the saints."

Now from verses 4 and 6 of Rev. 20, "they lived and reigned" and "Blessed and holy is he that hath part in the first resurrection... they shall reign," it is clear that all who rise in the first resurrection do reign, from which it certainly follows that such as are not accounted worthy to reign do not rise at that time. Who shall say to what large degree this searching, conscience-quickening belief contributed to the blamelessness of Mr. Chapman's beautiful life? The doctrine of the coming of our Lord is in the Scripture so set forth as to promote holiness of life (1 John 3:3; 2 Pet. 3:11-14; 1 Pet. 1:13). That line of exposition will be found most accordant with Scripture which makes the most imperative demand for holiness.

> To gain that prize I towards that goal will struggle
>   Which God has set before;
> To gain that prize 'gainst sin and death I'll battle
>   And with the world make war;
> And if it brings me here but shame and troubles
>   And scorn, if pain life fills,
> Yet seek I nothing of earth's empty baubles;
>   My God alone my longing stills.

To gain that prize, to reach that crown I'm pressing
    Which Christ doth ready hold;
I mean His great reward to be possessing,
    His booty for the bold.
I will not rest, no weariness shall stay me,
    To hasten home is best,
Where I some day in peace and joy shall lay me
    Upon my Saviour's heart and rest.
               (From the German).

3
The Period of the Parousia

The first resurrection, accompanied by the removal of the living, will take place at a certain moment when the Lord Himself shall descend from His present place at the right hand of the throne of God, in the upper heavens, to the neighbourhood of the earth (1 Thess. 4:15-17). He is now absent from the earth: then He will be present again. This will be the commencement of His Parousia (presence). The Word of God shows that this descent will take place at the end of that Great Tribulation which is to be inflicted upon the saints by the Beast at the very close of this age. It has been suggested that the phrase sat down on the right hand of the Majesty in the heights (Heb. 1:3) does not imply *place*, but merely dignity. Yet this will not be said of 1 Kin. 2:19: "The king sat down on his throne, and caused a throne to be set for the king's mother, and she sat on his right hand." There is a spot in the heaven of heavens where the Father is throned in light unapproachable by man in the flesh. There the Son sits at the right hand of God, and thence He will descend at the hour which the Father has set within his own authority.

1. Christ stated that a time would come when His enemies should "see the Son of man sitting at the right hand of power, and coming on the clouds of heaven" (Matt. 26:64): from which it would appear that down to an hour when He is to be seen by the godless at the right hand of power He remains there, which place therefore He did not leave for the air several years before that time. Christ had said before that the hour when the world should thus see Him would follow the Great Tribulation (Matt. 24:29-30).

2. Now under seal 6 (Rev. 6) the godless are shown fleeing in terror from the face of God and from the wrath of the Lamb and are hiding in the rocks. This accords with paragraph one above and with Isa. 2:10, 19, 21. The latter passage fixes the hour as that when "Jehovah ariseth to shake terribly the earth," again showing at what point

the Lord leaves the throne on high. Seal 6 repeats the many signs in heaven and earth which Christ said should follow the Tribulation (Matt. 24:29-30), which confirms that the "arising" of the Lord and the appearing of His glory to men follow that Tribulation.

3. According to Paul himself the "blessed hope" of the church is the "*appearing* of the *glory* of our great God and Saviour Jesus Christ" (Tit. 2:13), not any secret, invisible event. The words in italics are a repetition of words used by Christ on the same topic (Matt. 24:29-30). So that at the close of His then presence with His disciples the Lord pointed them onward to His appearing in glory, and they adopted that appearing as their hope. But the Lord stated that this His appearing would be after the signs that should immediately follow the Great Tribulation.

The suggestion that the "blessed hope" is a first event and the appearing a second is denied by the grammar of the passage in Greek. "Hope and appearing belong together" (Alford. See also Bloomfield, Conybeare, Weymouth, etc.). "'The blessed hope' is the appearing" (Speaker's Commentary).

4. The Lord stated next (Matt. 24:31) that at that moment of His appearing He would gather together His elect. That the elect are Christians, not Jews, is certain. (a) No gathering of Jews to Palestine at this hour is known to Scripture. There is to be one before the reign of the Beast, for he will persecute them there, and another, expressly termed the *second*, after Christ shall have come to Jerusalem (Isa. 11:10-12). If this at the moment of the appearing were of Jews that later one would be the third. (b) This gathering of the elect is universal: were it of Israelites none of these would be left for that later and second gathering. (c) The Gentile nations, not angels, will be agents of that second gathering of Israel (Isa. 11:12; 14:2; 49:22; 66:19-20). (d) This gathering takes place while Christ is yet in the clouds, whereas Israel are not to be gathered there, but to their land and city. (e) The term "elect" is applied to angels (1 Tim. 5:21) and to Christ (Lk. 13:35; 1 Pet. 2:6). "Election" is used of God's purpose concerning Jacob (Rom. 9:11). The cognate verb "chosen" is used of Jehovah's choice of Israel as His earthly people (Acts 13:17), of guests selecting the chief seats (Lk. 14:7), and of Mary choosing the good part

(Lk. 10:42). None of these places has any bearing upon the interpretation of Matt. 24:31 and Mk. 13:27: and in every other place of the many in the New Testament the invariable application of these terms is to Christians. Even in Rom. 11:5, 7, 28, though Israelites are in view, it is as Christians they form the "remnant according to the election of grace." Nothing arises to suggest that Christ meant the term in another sense to His former use in Luke 18:7, "shall not God do justice to His own elect," or for supposing that the Christians to whom the Gospels first came could think it to have any other than its by that time fixed application to Christians.

5. Christ further stated that the gathering of the elect should be accompanied by "a great sound of a trumpet" (Matt. 24:31). This is repeated in 1 Thess. 4:16, and 1 Cor. 15:52 describes this as the "last trump." The last trump of Scripture is recorded in Rev. 11:15-18. Under it four events are grouped: (i) The anger of the nations and God's wrath upon them; (ii) The time of the dead to be judged—the godly dead, for it is before the millennium: comp. Dan. 7:22; (iii) The rewarding of the prophets, saints, and those who fear God; (iv) The destruction of the destroyers of the earth.

Thus the raising and rewarding of the godly take place at the same epoch as the destruction of the wicked, and all is after the Tribulation, for it is the time of the destruction of the Beast, and is after he has persecuted, and has killed the Two Witnesses in Jerusalem (Rev. 11:1-13).

6. This is confirmed by the declaration of the strong angel whose message follows trumpet 6 (Rev. 10:5-7). He announces that the mystery of God shall be completed during the period of the seventh trumpet. Paul taught concerning: (i) the *mystery* (secret); (ii) that it was *according to the gospel* (good tidings); (iii) that it was made known according to the *commandment of the eternal God;* (iv) and that this was done through the writings *of the prophets* (Rom. 16:25-27). The angel repeats these four particulars concerning (i) the *mystery;* (ii) that it was *according to the good tidings* (the same word as gospel); (iii) that it was *declared by God;* (iv) through His servants *the prophets.* The two passages read thus:

Rom. 16:25-27: "Now unto Him that is able to establish you according to my *gospel* and the preaching of Jesus Christ, according to the revelation of the *mystery* which hath been kept in silence through times eternal, but now is manifested, and by the *scriptures of the prophets*, according to the *commandment of the eternal God*, is made known unto all the nations unto obedience of faith...."

Rev. 10:7: "... in the days of the voice of the seventh angel, when he is about to sound, then is finished the *mystery* of God, according to the *good tidings* which *He declared* to His servants *the prophets*."

The attempt to make out that these are not the same mystery, and that there are two divine purposes of which all four particulars are equally and separately true, will surely only be made in the interests of some special theory of interpretation.

The mystery that was such a vital element in apostolic teaching is shown by Eph. 3:1-13 to be the gathering of the church from Jews and Gentiles, and therefore was it to be made known unto all the nations. This work will be completed by the resurrection and rapture, which will be under trumpet 7, which will be after the Tribulation, as shown above under (5).

7. Other Scriptures also reveal this same grouping of events. In 2 Thess. 1:6-8, it is said that the delivering of the saints from trouble at the hands of the godless will be at the time of the destruction of the latter by the Lord at His revelation in flaming fire with His angels. Thus the church of God is viewed as continuing in affliction right down to the apocalypse (public appearing) of Christ.

1 Thess. 4:13-18 and 5:1-11 belong together, though often arbitrarily dissevered, and they similarly associate these events for the godly and the godless respectively. The "times and the seasons" of verse 1 necessarily means the times and the seasons in which will come the events just mentioned. No other events have been mentioned, so that there is no other antecedent to the expression, which thus connects the paragraphs.

Thus the earliest revelations by Christ, the middle period teachings of Paul and others (see 2 Pet. 3:15, that Peter and Paul taught alike), and the latest through John (Rev. 10:11), agree.

The Period of the Parousia 39

8. This harmony is seen further in the passages which picture the Lord as coming as a thief.

Christ used the figure to warn His own servants of His own household (Matt. 24:42, 44: Lk. 12:39). Peter, who heard that warning, repeats it to those who had "obtained like precious faith" with himself "in the righteousness of our God and Saviour Jesus Christ" (2 Pet. 3:10, 11; 1:1). Paul reminds the Thessalonians that they, by his particular instruction, knew of that thief-like coming, and so they need not be caught unawares by its unannounced arrival, only they must be very careful to keep awake, *continuing watchful and sober* (1 Thess. 5:21). The Lord from heaven repeats these warnings to the church at Sardis (Rev. 3:3), plainly declaring that it is possible for Christians to cease to watch (comp. Mk. 13:36), and so to be overtaken by that day as a thief. Finally, just as wicked spirits are gathering the armies of the Beast for the final battle with the Lamb at His return, the Lord interjects the announcement, "Behold, I come as a thief" (Rev. 16:15). This were a singularly inappropriate place for the renewal of this warning if in fact the coming as a thief had taken place long previously at a supposed coming of the Lord before the end days entirely.

Thus it appears that the "house," and the Lord's servants in it, continue on earth in His absence down to the close of the Tribulation era when the Beast is preparing for the final battle.

9. That the first resurrection takes place after the Tribulation is clear from the fact that those martyred by the Beast share therein (Rev. 20:4). The supposition that this resurrection will be completed in stages, of which this will be the last, is not needed and seems without Scripture authority.

10. In Rev. 14 there is a series of six visions. In the first a company of saints are seen on the Mount Zion with the Lamb, in the region of the throne of God, for the elders and the living creatures are present, before the throne.[1] These saints have been "purchased

---

1. In Revelation "before the throne" always means a heavenly locality, not on earth. It is the place of the presence of God, of the elders, living creatures, angels, the glassy sea, the heavenly throne and altar. See 4:5, 6, 10; 7:9; 8:3; 14:3; 20:12; all its occurrences.

out of the earth" (showing that they are not then on earth), and they learn the song of heaven. In the second vision the hour of judgment strikes; that is, the end days begin. In the third we learn that the Harlot, Babylon, has been destroyed, which vision is amplified in ch. 17. In the fourth the Great Tribulation is contemplated, for the Beast is persecuting. After this the fifth vision shows: (i) The Son of man now on the clouds, having therefore come down from Mount Zion. (ii) His angels (the sickle, comp. Matt. 13:39) are gathering up from the earth His "harvest," the ripened saints He has grown as wheat, and will gather into His barn in safety. The sixth and last vision pictures the destruction of the Beast and his armies, which is further shown in ch. 19:11-21.

Here again the presence on the clouds, with the gathering up of the godly, is put between the Tribulation and the destruction of the lawless. With unique emphasis Christ had taught that the "wheat" *must* remain in the field with the "tares" "until the harvest" and that the harvest is the "consummation of the age" (Matt. 13:30 - 39), not any point of time prior to the End Days. In Rev. 14 this harvest is shown appropriately as the last great event but one in this age.

The whole New Testament agrees in putting at this point the appearing in glory of the Son of man, which was seen from afar by Old Testament prophets; nor does the Scripture know of any earlier descent of the Lord from the throne to the air. And so Paul in one sentence (2 Thess. 2:1-5) grouped together (a) the Parousia, (b) our gathering together unto the Lord, and (c) the Day of the Lord, and most expressly announced and warned that these all must be preceded by the apostasy and the revelation of the Man of Sin. George Müller said: "having been a careful diligent student of the Bible for nearly fifty years, my mind has long been settled upon this point, and I have not the shadow of a doubt about it. The Scripture declares plainly that the Lord Jesus will not come until the apostasy shall have taken place, and the man of sin, the 'son of perdition' (or personal Antichrist) shall have been revealed, as seen in 2 Thess. 2."

4
The Pre-Tribulation Rapture

There are two principal views upon the matters here considered: one, that the Parousia will commence prior to the Times of the End, and that at its inception all believers of the heavenly calling, dead and living, will be taken to the presence of the Lord in the air; the other, that the Parousia will occur at the close of the Great Tribulation, until when no believers will be raised or changed. The one view says that no believers will go into the End Times, the other that none then living will escape them. The one involves that the utmost measure of unfaithfulness or carnality in a believer puts him in no peril of forfeiting the supreme honour of rapture or of having to endure the dread End Days: the other view involves that no degree of faithfulness or of holiness will enable a saint to escape those Days. As regards *this* matter, godliness and unfaithfulness seem immaterial on either view; which raises a doubt of both views.

Our study thus far has shown that the former view is unfounded: we have now to see that the latter is partly right and partly wrong. It is right in asserting that the Parousia will commence at the close of the Great Tribulation, but wrong in declaring that no saints living as the End Times near will escape that awful period.

1. For our Lord Jesus Christ has declared distinctly that escape is possible. In Luke 21 is a record of instruction given by Him to four apostles on the Mount of Olives. It is a parallel report to Matt. 24 and 25 and Mark 13, and it deals specifically with the Times of the End and His Parousia. He foretold great international wars, accompanied with earthquakes, famines, and pestilences, to be followed by terrors and great signs from heaven (vv. 10, 11: comp. Seals 1-4, Rev. 6). These things are to be preceded by a general persecution of His followers (ver. 12), which will be the first indication that the End Days are at hand. Then Jerusalem is to be trodden down by the Gentiles right on until the Times of the Gentiles run out (ver. 24:

comp. Rev. 11:2 where the same term "trodden down" is used, and Zech. 14:1-5). This shows that it is the End-times of which Christ is speaking, as is further shown by His earlier statement that at that time of vengeance "*all* things that are written" shall be fulfilled. *All* things that are written in the prophets concerning Jerusalem, Israel, and the Gentiles were not by any means fulfilled at the destruction of Jerusalem in A.D. 70.

Then He mentions the disturbances in nature and the fears of mankind that are grouped under seal 6 in Rev. 6:12-17, and adds explicitly that "*then* shall they see the Son of Man coming in a cloud with power and great glory," and that when these things begin His disciples may know that their redemption draweth nigh (ver. 27, 28).

In concluding this outline of the period of the Beast the Lord then uttered this exhortation and promise: "But take heed to yourselves, lest haply your hearts be overcharged with surfeiting, and drunkenness, and cares of this life, and that day come on you suddenly as a snare: for so shall it come upon all them that dwell on the face of all the earth. But watch ye at every season, making supplication, that ye may prevail to escape all these things that shall come to pass, and to stand before the Son of Man."

This declares distinctly: (1) That escape is possible from all those things of which Christ had been speaking, that is, from the whole End-times. (2) That that day of testing will be universal, and inevadable by any then on the earth, which involves the removal from the earth of any who are to escape it. (3) That those who are to escape will be taken to where He, the Son of Man, will then be, that is, at the throne of the Father in the heavens. They will stand before Him there. (4) That there is a fearful peril of disciples becoming worldly of heart and so being enmeshed in that last period. (5) That hence it is needful to watch, and to pray ceaselessly, that so we may prevail over all obstacles and dangers and thus escape that era.

This most important and unequivocal statement by our Lord sets aside the opinion that all Christians will escape irrespective of their moral state, and also negatives the notion that no escape is possible. There is a door of escape; but as with all doors, only those who are awake will see it, and only those who are in earnest will reach it ere the storm bursts. In every place in the New Testament the word "escape" has its natural force—*ekpheugō*, to flee out of a place of trouble and be quite clear thereof.[1] It never means to endure the trial successfully. In this very discourse of the Lord it is in contrast with the statement, "He that endureth (*hupomenō*) to the end [of these things] the same shall be saved" (Matt. 24:13). One escapes, another endures.

The attempt to evade the application of this passage to Christians on the plea that it refers to "Jewish" disciples of Christ, is baseless: (a) No "Jewish" disciples of Christ are known to the Scriptures (Gal. 3:28; Eph. 2:14-18). (b) The God-fearing remnant of Israel of the End-days will in no wise escape these things that shall come to pass (Mal. 3:14; Zech. 13:8-9; Jer. 30:7-8). (c) Nor will they believe on Jesus as their Messiah until they see Him coming in glory (Zech. 12:9-10, 13:6; Matt. 23:39). (d) The assertion that the title Son of Man is "Jewish" is equally unwarranted, for the term "man" is necessarily universal to the race, and does not belong peculiarly to any one nation. (Comp. John 3:14-15; 5:25-29: "whosoever" and "all").

2. In harmony with this utterance of our Lord is His further statement to the church at Philadelphia (Rev. 3:10): "Because thou didst keep the word of My patience, I also will keep thee from (*ek*) the hour of trial, that hour which is to come upon the whole inhabited earth, to try them that dwell upon the earth." Here also are declared: (a) The universality of that hour of trial, so that any escape from it must involve removal; (b) the promise of being kept from it; (c) the intimation that such preservation is the consequence of a certain moral condition: "*Because* thou didst keep... I also will keep." As this is addressed to a church, no question of a "Jewish" application can arise. Nor do known facts or the Scriptures allow of the supposition that every Christian keeps the word of Christ's patience (Matt. 24:12; Rev. 2:5: Gal. 6:12; Col. 4:14 with 2 Tim.

---

1. It comes only at Luke 21:36; Acts 16:27; 19:16; Rom. 2:3; 2 Cor. 11:33; 1 Thess. 5:3; Heb. 2:3; 12:25. In comparison with Rom. 2:3, see its use in the LXX in the interpolated passage after Esth. 8:13: "they suppose that they shall escape the sin-hating vengeance of the ever-seeing God"; also Judg. 6:11; Job. 15:30; Prov. 10:19; 12:13. The sense is invariably as stated above.

4:10 concerning Demas); so that this promise cannot be stretched to mean all believers.

In *The Bible Treasury*, 1865, p. 380, there is an instructive note by J. N. Darby (see also Coll. Writings, vol. 13, Critical I, 581) on the difference between *apo* and *ek*. The former regards hostile *persons* and being delivered from them; the latter refers to a *state* and being kept from getting into it. On Rev. 3:10 he wrote: "So in Rev. 3 the faithful are kept from getting into this state, preserved from getting into it. or, as we say, kept out of it. For the words here answer fully to the English 'out of' or 'from'." That the thought is not being kept from being injured in soul by the trials is implied in the expression "Keep thee out of *that hour*"; it is from the period of time itself that the faithful are to be kept, not merely from its spiritual perils.

3. Of this escape and preservation there are two pictures as there are two promises.

In Rev. 12 is a vision of (a) a woman; (b) a man-child whom she bears; (c) the rest of her family. Light on this complex figure may be gained from Hosea 4 and Isa. 49:17-21; 50:1. Israel and Zion, viewed as corporate systems in continuity, are a "woman," a "mother"; individual Israelites at any one time are the "children." This usage is the same as when an individual Romanist calls the church his "mother." The "mother" is that system continuing through the centuries; yet in one sense, the woman at a given hour is composed of her children.

As to this "woman" the dominant fact is that at one and the same time she is seen in heaven arrayed with heavenly glory and on earth in sorrow and pain. This simultaneous and contradictory experience is true of the church of God only (comp. Eph. 2:6 with 3:13 and 6:10-13; and 1 Pet. 1:3-5 with vv. 6, 7). In Scripture Israel corporately has no standing in the heavens: her destiny and glory are earthly. The national divisions of earth do not continue in heaven.

As to the Man-child, his birth and rapture, as with the whole of this book from c. 4:1, pointed to events which the angel distinctly said were future to the time of the visions. There is no exception to this, and therefore there is no possible reference to the resurrection and ascension of Christ. Nor, in the fact, did our Lord at His birth escape from Satan by rapture to the throne of God: on the contrary, the Dragon slew Him in manhood and only thereafter did He ascend to heaven. Nor at the ascension of Christ was Satan cast out of heaven. Thirty years later, when Paul wrote to the Ephesians, he and his servants were still there (Eph. 6:12), and another thirty years later again, when John saw the visions, his ejection was still future (Rev. 12).

The identity of this Man-child is indicated by the statement that he "is to rule all the nations with a rod of iron," for this is a repetition of the promise (Rev. 2:26-27), "And he that overcometh, and he that keepeth My works unto the end [comp. the keeping the word of My patience, as above], to him will I give authority over the nations, and he shall rule them with a rod of iron." This promise is given only to Christ and the overcomers of the churches. As it cannot here (Rev. 12) apply to Him it can only apply to them.

This removal of the Man-child cannot be the event foretold in 1 Thess. 4:15-17, for those there in view will be taken up only as far as to the air around this earth when the Lord descends thereto from heaven, but this removal takes the Man-child to the throne of God, which is where Christ now is, in the upper heavens. This fulfils the promise that such as prevail to escape shall "stand before the Son of Man."

As we have seen, the Lord does not descend from heaven till the close of the Great Tribulation, not before Satan is cast down. Moreover, this one child can be only a part of the whole family, not the completed church in view in 1 Thess. 4[2] and 1 Cor. 15. The "woman" out of whom he is born remains on earth, and after his ascent the "rest of her seed" are persecuted by the Beast; but his removal is before the Beast is even on the scene or Satan is cast

---

2. In 1 Thess. 4:15, 17 the word *perileipō*, "that are left," deserves notice. It is not found elsewhere in the New Testament, but the force may be seen in the LXX of Amos. 5:15, and of the verb (in some editions) at 2 Chron. 34:21; Hag. 2:3. In each case it means, to be left after others are gone. So the lexicons also, and they are confirmed by *The Vocabulary of the Greek Testament*. In this place it seems redundant save on our view that the rapture there in question is at the close of the Tribulation and that some saints will not have been left on earth until that event, but will have been removed alive earlier; for to have marked the contrast with those that had died it would have been enough to have said "we that are alive," without twice repeating this unusual word.

out of heaven. Thus those who will form this company escape all things that will occur in the End-times, as Christ promised; and the identification with the overcomers declares that they had lived that watchful, prayerful, victorious life, upon which, as the Lord said, that escape will depend.

Consequent upon this removal of the watchful, Satan is cast out of heaven, and presently brings up the Beast, who persecutes the rest of the woman's family (12:17, 18; 13:7-10). So that one section of the family escapes the End-times by being rapt to heaven, and the rest, the more numerous portion, as the term indicates, go into the Great Tribulation. These latter are such as "keep the commandments of God and hold the testimony of Jesus" (ver. 17). In Rev. 14:12, such are termed "the saints," which in New Testament times, was the term regularly used by Christians of one another; and among their number John had already included himself (1:2, 9). It covers therefore the church of God, of which he was a leader.

4. The second picture of this pre-Tribulation rapture is given in Rev. 14. In this chapter there are six scenes:

i. "Firstfruits" with the Lamb on the Mount Zion (1-6).
ii. The hour of judgment commences (6, 7).
iii. "Babylon" is announced as having fallen (8).
iv. The Beast period is present and persecution is in progress (9-13).
v. The Son of Man on a white cloud reaps His "harvest" (14-16).
vi. The "vintage" of the earth is gathered, and is trodden in the winepress on earth (17-20).

The agricultural figure wrought into this chapter by the Holy Spirit is the key to its teaching. In the early summer the Jew was to gather a sheaf of corn as soon as enough was ripe, and this was to be presented to God in the temple at Jerusalem as "firstfruits" (Lev. 23:9-14). After some time (ver. 15) the whole of the fields would be ripened by the great summer heat and the whole harvest would be reaped. But this, though removed indeed from the fields where it had grown, would not be taken so far as to the temple, but only to the granary on the farm. Then the season closed with the vintage, and the clusters were not taken away from where they had grown, the winepress being in the vineyard and the grapes being crushed therein.

Thus the "firstfruits" are shown as on Mount Zion with the Lamb, the "harvest" is taken only as far as to the clouds, which accords with 1 Thess. 4; and the vintage is trodden outside the city of Jerusalem, where the armies of Antichrist are camped.

The last scene is the destruction of the Beast by the Lord at His descent to Jerusalem (Rev. 19:15). Next prior to that event is the removal of the elect to the clouds: immediately before this is the period of the Tribulation: preceding that is the destruction of the harlot system of Rev. 17 (see ver. 16-18): this event follows first upon the striking of the hour of divine judgment: but before any of those things of the End commence the Firstfruits are seen with the Lamb in heaven, as He promised (Lk. 21:36).

The Firstfruits *cannot* be a picture of the whole of the redeemed as they will finally appear at the end of the drama of those days, for firstfruits *cannot* be more than a portion of the whole harvest, neither can *first*fruits describe the *final* ingathering. It were a contradiction to speak thus. Firstfruits *must* be gathered first, before the reaping of the remainder. The number 144,000 need not be taken literally. In the Apocalypse numbers are sometimes literal, but sometimes figurative.

As has been noted above, these had been purchased *out of* the earth, which shows that they were not then on earth, and they learn the song of the heavenly choir. Nor can this Mount Zion be at Jerusalem, but must be that in the heavens, for the Lord will not descend to the earthly Zion till after the Tribulation, not before it, as this scene is placed.

The 144,000 of ch. 7 are a different company. They are the godly Remnant of Israel seen on earth after the Appearing and the gathering of the elect to the clouds, and are sealed (comp. Ezek. 9) so as to be untouched by the wrath of the Lamb now to be poured upon the godless (Zeph. 2:3; Isa. 26:20, 21).

The identity of these Firstfruits is revealed by a similar means to that which reveals the identity of the Man-child. These persons are shown as connected with the Father, the Lamb, and the Mount Zion, which also refers back to the promises to the overcomers, and shows that the Firstfruits will be a portion of the company of the victors, who, it is promised, will be marked as connected with the Father, the Son, and the New Jerusalem (Rev. 3:12). These three marks of identification come together in these two passages only. Now the moral features attributed to these Firstfruits show that they had lived just that pure, faithful Christian life which necessarily results from watchfulness, prayerfulness, and patient obedience to the words of Christ, as inculcated in the corresponding passages quoted.

As the Man-child and the rest of the woman's seed were but one family, only removed in two portions, one before the Beast and the other after his persecutions, so firstfruits and harvest were grown from one sowing in one field, only they were reaped in two portions, one before the hour of judgment and the other after the Beast had persecuted. We have remarked above that these latter are termed "saints," and that this was the regular title that Christians gave to one another; that it is amplified by the double description "they that keep the commandments of God and the faith of Jesus," and that in this description John had before twice included himself; so that the terms mean that company in which John had membership, the church of God. Moreover, as the Jewish remnant will not have owned Jesus during the period in view the terms can apply only to Christians.

Finally, as between the gathering of the sheaf of firstfruits and the ingathering of the harvest there came the intensest summer heat, so between the removal of the Firstfruits and the reaping of the Harvest there is placed (ver. 9-13) the Great Tribulation, that final persecution which while, like all persecution, it will wither the unrooted stalk (Matt. 13:21), ripens the matured grain. It is ripeness, not the calendar or the clock, that determines the time of reaping (Mk. 4:29). The Heavenly Husbandman reaps no unripe grain: hence, "the hour to reap is come" when the harvest is "dried up" (Rev. 14:15), for the dryness of the kernel in the husk is its fitness for the garner and for use. Thus the Great Tribulation will be a true mercy to the Lord's people by fully developing and sanctifying them for their heavenly destiny and glory.

It thus appears that the foretold order of events will be:

1. The removal of such as prevail to escape the Times of the End. These will be taken up to God and to His throne on the Mount Zion, not to the air. Nor does the Lord come for them; they are simply taken, like Enoch or Elijah: taken to stand before Him and His throne. Nor is a resurrection announced for this moment. The dead, because dead, will have escaped the End-times, which escape is the announced object of this rapture.

2. The Beast arises and persecutes.

3. The Lord descends to the clouds and gathers together His elect (Matt. 24:29–31; 1 Cor. 15:51, 52; 1 Thess. 4:15-17; Tit. 2:13; Rev. 14:14-16). At this time there will be the first resurrection. Each who shall be accounted worthy of the coming age will "arise into his lot at the *end of the days,*" not sooner, certainly not before the End days have commenced (Dan. 12:13). Nor may we assume of the Firstfruits that they will have priority in the Kingdom over equally faithful saints of earlier times.

4. After an interval the Lord descends to the Mount of Olives, destroys the Beast and his armies, and establishes the Kingdom of the heavens on the earth.

It is therefore our wisdom to give earnest, unremitting attention to our Lord's most solemn exhortation "take heed to yourselves, lest haply your hearts be overcharged with surfeiting and drunkenness [that is, fleshly indulgence], and cares of this life [that is, its burdens through either poverty or riches], and that day come on you suddenly as a snare: for so shall it come on all them that dwell on the face of all the earth. But watch ye at every season, making supplication, that ye may prevail to escape all these things that shall come to pass, and to stand before the Son of Man (Lk. 21:34-36).

> Oh, dare and suffer all things!
> Yet but a stretch of road,
> Then wondrous words of welcome,
> And then—the FACE OF GOD!

Many of the perplexities felt as to these themes are caused by misconceptions upon three subjects—the constitution of man, the place and state of the dead, the judgment of the Lord upon His people. Some discussion of these matters follows.

5

An Enquiry as to Man's Constitution and Future, with Remarks on Hades and Paradise

As treasures heavy and valuable may hang upon a small hook, so consequences weighty and far-reaching may follow the settlement of what may seem a small point.

Because at death the spirit of man returns to God who gave it (Eccl. 12:7), it is generally thought that man goes then to God in heaven. If the passage meant this it would teach that the ungodly, as well as the godly, go to heaven at death, for it refers to man as man. This alone shows that this is not the sense of the passage. But further, the meaning given assumes that the man, the conscious entity, the person, the ego, is his spirit. But if this is not so, then the opinion stated has no support in Scripture.

Again, many annihilationists deem that the man, the person, consists of two parts only, the body and the spirit, and that when these are parted at death the person, the conscious ego, ceases to exist until the two parts are reunited in resurrection. But if the conscious personality has ceased to exist, it is extremely difficult to conceive that it is the identical conscious person that comes into existence again. Would it not rather be a new personality that comes into being at resurrection? How can continuity of personality persist during non-existence, and how, then, shall this new man be held morally responsible for the deeds of that former person, and be righteously liable to judgment therefor?

Moreover, this would involve (what indeed we have heard asserted) a disintegration of the person of the Man, Christ Jesus, between His death and resurrection. According to the theory, during that period His humanity was non-existent. So that whilst the Son of

God existed, *Christ* did not until resurrection. This is fatal heresy, and alone forbids the doctrine in question.

The alternative must be for the annihilationist to adopt the first mentioned view, that personality attaches to the spirit, as others of that school do. But if it be, that the *soul* is the person, and that after death the soul has its own separate existence, then the whole assertion fails.

Inasmuch therefore as most serious issues are involved, this inquiry is of great practical importance. Indeed, it may be said that many most interesting and profitable themes can only be understood aright by a right understanding of our question: Soul or Spirit, Which is the Man?

It must here be remarked that this theme, like all such profounder topics of the Word of God, *cannot* be studied in the English Authorised Version. It is not possible, on account of the deliberate irregularity in translation used by the translators so as to secure pleasing English. We quote here generally the English Revised Version, and sometimes the New Translation of J. N. Darby (Morrish, London). This, one of the earliest individual translations, remains, in our opinion, by far the most helpful of all such.

1. The Creation of Man

The creation of man is described in Gen. 2:7: "And Jehovah Elohim formed man, dust of the ground, and breathed into his nostrils the breath of life; and man became a living soul."

Here are three stages. 1. A material form fashioned but of material particles, dust. This is the body. 2. A somewhat inbreathed by God, named in Eccl. 12:7, "spirit." That the "breath" of Gen. 2:7, and the "spirit" of Eccl. 12:7 are one is confirmed by the combination of the two terms in Gen. 7:22: "All in whose nostrils was the *breath* of the *spirit* of life." 3. The result, that man became what is here called "soul," a living soul.

1. As to the body, it is to be observed that it was not itself the *man*. *It* lay there, fashioned and prepared, but the *man* was not yet there. The body was an inanimate form, which preceded the existence of

the man. This as against the Sadducean materialist and his assertion that the body is the man, and that when it dies his existence ends.

2. The same is true of the breath or spirit, which God inbreathed. It also was in existence prior to the man, for God breathed it into the body. It was not God; it is not divine: it is not said that God breathed of Himself, or breathed His Spirit into the body, but a somewhat not to be defined by us as to its substance or nature, but which God terms "spirit." In Zech. 12:1 it is declared to be a created thing, a thing "formed," as an article made by a potter. It is the same word as "potter" in Zech. 11:13, and is found first at Gen. 2:8, God "formed man." This as against the pantheist, and the doctrine akin to pantheism, that there is a measure of divinity in all men by creation. The immanence of God in all creation is truth, the identity of all things, or of any created thing, with God is error, deadly error.

Thus the spirit was not the man, for *he* only came into existence by reason of the inbreathing of the spirit into the body, which conjunction of two separate, previously existing things, resulted in the creation of a third: "man became a living soul."

3. It remains only that the man is what he is here described to be, "a living soul." The man is the soul, not the spirit, even as he is not the body. This as against the annihilationist theory above mentioned.

It is fairly certain that every false philosophy that has beclouded the thoughts of man had been instilled into men's minds by spirits of darkness in Babylon before Moses wrote Genesis, and had thence infected all races. In that case he would have been instructed in them in Egypt among the rest of its learning; and when he was re-instructed by the God of truth, he so described the creation of the universe, and of man in particular, as to deny every false idea current then or since.

This threefold composition of man is implied everywhere in the Word of God, and sometimes is distinctly stated. Thus in 1 Thess. 5:3: "And the God of peace himself sanctify you wholly; and may your spirit and soul and body be preserved entire, without blame in the parousia of our Lord Jesus Christ." The body is distinguished from the spirit in James 2:26: "The body apart from (the) spirit is dead"; and the soul from the spirit in Heb. 4:12, "The word of God. .. piercing to the dividing of soul and spirit."

The man has a body with which he operates upon the material world; but the body is not the man. He has also a spirit with which he has dealings with the spiritual realm; but the spirit is not the man. The man himself, the conscious ego, is the soul. Personality in man inheres in the soul, which will become yet more apparent as we proceed, but may be seen in such passages as Ex. 1:5: "all the *souls* were seventy *souls*"; Lev. 4:2: "if a *soul* shall sin" 5:2: "if a *soul* touch"; Lev. 5:4: "if a *soul* swear" 7:18: "the *soul* that eateth", etc., etc. The evident sense is: "If a *person*" do this or that. See also LXX Ezk. 16:5.

2. The Meaning of the Word Death

Now "the body without spirit is dead" (Jas. 2:26), and the soul, the man, cannot use or inhabit a dead body. The spirit imparts to the body vitality, animation, and makes it usable by man. Thus so long as the two are united man is a living soul, but when God recalls the spirit which He gave, the body ceases to have life, the soul vacates it, and thenceforth, until resurrection, the man is dead.

But it is carefully and always to be remembered that in Scripture the term "life" does not mean simply existence, but much more and much rather it means a certain mode or quality of existence, and equally so the term "death," therefore, does not mean non-existence, but an opposite state or mode of existence. Many things exist which do not exhibit the property called "life." All annihilationist reasoning which we have read assumes this false sense of the words "life" and "death" and cannot proceed without it.

Yet in some real sense Adam died the day he disobeyed God, according to the sentence, "in the day that thou eatest of it thou shalt certainly die" (Gen. 2:17), but he did not cease to exist that day. So, by a powerful antithesis, it is said, "she that giveth herself to pleasure is *dead* while she liveth," which cannot be read, ceases to exist while she exists (1 Tim. 5:6). In much the same way we speak of a living death.

Equally arresting is our Lord's argument against the annihilationists of His day (Lk. 20:37-38).

He first admits that Abraham, Isaac, and Jacob are dead, saying, "But that the *dead* are raised," and at once adds that "God is not the God of the dead, but of the *living,* for all live unto Him." So dead in one sense, they are yet alive in another, showing that both terms describe only relative conditions of existence. Similarly the Lord makes the father of the prodigal say: "This my son was dead, and is alive again" (Lk. 15:24), though in another sense he had been as much alive in the far country as after his return. Further, it is clear that the first death does not cause the annihilation of the sinner or there could be no second death for him.

Thus the word death does not of itself mean ceasing to be, and such as say that the second death means annihilation are bound to show that the Scripture adds to the word this sense which does not belong to it. The second death is the "lake of fire" (Rev. 20:14). The beast and the false prophet are cast thereinto before the thousand years reign of Christ (Rev. 19:20); they are still there at the close of that period when Satan is cast there (Rev. 20:10); so that a thousand years in the second death has not destroyed their existence, and the sentence upon all three is that "they shall be tormented day and night for the ages of the ages." It would be impossible to torment that which had ceased to be.

It is consistent with the holiness and the love of God—for it is fact—that angels that abused His favour shall be confined in that place of misery, Tartarus, for already thousands of years (2 Pet. 2:4); that Dives (Lk. 16), who abused His goodness on earth, shall be *tormented* in a flame in Hades for a period unknown to us, for it is not yet ended; that the Beast and the false prophet, who blasphemed His holy name, shall be in the lake of fire for more than a thousand years at least. As this is consistent with the love and justice of God why should it not be so for 10,000 years, for 100,000, for a billion years, or for ever, and especially in the case of those who rejected His amazing love in Christ, trampled under foot the Son of God, and definitely resisted the Spirit of truth? We are not competent to form our own opinion as to what God may or may not, do consistently with His character and because of it. We can only bow to what He has revealed, assured that He will ever act consistently with what

He is, for He is not able to do otherwise. We can best estimate what sentence a judge may pass by considering what sentences he has before passed, as well as what statements he may have made as to future sentences.

3. WHAT TAKES PLACE AT DEATH?

The passage before cited tells us that "the *dust* returns to the earth as it was, and the *spirit* returns unto God who gave it" (Eccl. 12:7). But what becomes of the *soul*?

An actual case is better than much speculation, an ounce of fact being worth a ton of theory. Of the Man Christ Jesus we are told distinctly what took place at His death.

1. His dead *body* was laid in the tomb.

2. His last words on the cross were, "Father, into thy hands I commend my *spirit*" (Lk. 23:46), the human spirit thus returning unto God who gave it. That the human spirit is not the divine Spirit is seen clearly in the case of our Lord, for His entire holy humanity was a created thing conceived by an operation of the Holy Spirit in Mary (Lk. 1:35); years later it was anointed with power by the Spirit of God coming upon it; and at last on the cross, He surrendered His human spirit to the Father: an act impossible in relation to the Spirit of God with Whom He as God was in indissoluble union. The distinction—necessary and unavoidable—between the human and the divine is thus ever maintained. It was the human spirit which vitalized His body that Jesus gave up that He might die.

3. But the Spirit of prophecy in David (Ps. 16:10) had put into Messiah's mouth these other words: "Thou wilt not leave my *soul* to *Sheol*," which words were later, on the day of Pentecost, applied by Peter to Christ. "Thou wilt not leave my soul unto Hades" (Acts 2:27).

The error of Apollinaris (cent. 4), that the person of Christ consisted of a human body and soul only, with the divine Spirit (or Logos) taking the place in Him of a human spirit, must be steadfastly resisted. His humanity, as ours, consisted of body, soul, and spirit.

Sheol and Hades are equivalent words in Hebrew and Greek respectively. Of this region there is abundant information in

Scripture. It is very far from the fact, as spiritualists assert, that no certain information as to the state after death is available save what they think they receive from spirits through mediums. But most unfortunately the reader of the Authorized Version is completely stopped from this study by the variety of the terms employed. Sheol and Hades are rendered "grave," "pit," and "hell." The last in its older English meaning was not inaccurate, but it has come now to mean only the final place of the lost, the lake of fire, which never is the sense of Sheol or Hades. However, any diligent reader can pursue the subject in the Revised Version, for these original terms are given in either text or margin where ever they occur. This is one example, and an important one, of the superiority of the R.V. over the A.V.

4. WHERE IS HADES?

So the soul of our Lord was in Hades between His death and His resurrection on the third day. And Eph. 4:9-10 shows beyond question (1) that the "soul" was the Lord Himself, the personality, and (2) where Hades is situated. It says: "Having ascended up on high he has led captivity captive, and has given gifts unto men. Now this, having ascended, what is it but that He also descended into the lower parts of the earth? He that descended is the same who has also ascended far above all heavens, that he might fill all things."

1. The Person that ascended is the same Person that had descended, and from His own express words to Mary directly after His resurrection it is certain that He himself did not go to the Father at the hour of death, for He said to her: "I have (perf. ind., *anabebeeko*) not yet ascended to my Father; but go to my brethren and say unto them, I ascend to my Father" (Jo. 20:17). As His ascent to the Father had yet to take place it is clear that His human spirit, which He had commended to His Father as He died, was not *Himself*. Nor would the words admit the thought; for a man cannot send his personality, his self, away from himself, but we read of Jesus that "he gave up the spirit," or, *breathed out* the spirit, expired, as we say, the exact reversal of the act of creation when God *breathes in* the spirit.

The spirit therefore was not Himself, but a part of His composite humanity that He could dismiss by an act of the will. Man does not possess the power to do this; he must use violence to terminate his life: but Christ had received this power specially from His Father, according to His statement that the Father had given Him authority to lay down His life by His own act (Jo. 10:17-18).

2. The realm to which Christ descended, elsewhere, as we have seen, named Hades, is in this place in Ephesians stated plainly to be in "the lower parts of the earth." Scripture always locates it there and nowhere else. So Jacob of old said: "I will go *down* to Sheol to my son" (Gen. 37:35); and so the great prophet Samuel, when permitted by God to come from the world of the dead to announce the doom of Saul (an exceptional permission and event) said: "Why hast thou disquieted me to bring me *up?*" (1 Sam. 28:15). And so Christ said of Capernaum: "Shalt thou be exalted unto heaven? thou shalt go *down* unto Hades" (Matt. 11:23). As certainly as heaven is above the surface of the earth so certainly is Hades in the opposite direction.

Readers of the great classics will not need to be reminded that it was the common belief of the ancient world that the place of the dead was within the earth. We are not aware that any other opinion was then in men's minds. Their details of that place and its conditions are not to be accepted without Scripture confirmation, even as those of mediaeval writers like Dante are not to be; but the general facts of the location of the world of the dead within the earth, and of its having two divided regions, one of pain and one of bliss, are plainly adopted in Holy Scripture (as in Lk. 16), and so are confirmed as facts. And it could be shown that some details also are thus confirmed; as that the poets made visitors to and from that realm go and come through some cave or opening in the earth, and the Revelation similarly represents demon hordes as coming from the abyss through a shaft or opening therefrom (Rev. 9:1-11). We take the idea in each case to represent the conception that the realm of the dead is within the earth.

5. But Do Not Saints at Death "Go to Heaven"?

The death of Stephen presents the exact features seen at the death of his Lord. We are told that "he called upon the Lord, saying, Lord Jesus, receive my spirit... and... he fell asleep" (Acts 7:59,

60). His body did not fall asleep: it was battered to death by brutal ill-usage, and devout men buried it. It does not say that his spirit fell asleep, but that he surrendered it to his Lord. We shall see later that neither does the soul "sleep" in relation to that other realm to which it goes at death; so that the expression "fell asleep" can only mean as to its relation to this earth-life which it leaves at death.

But did not Stephen "go to heaven" when he died? Do not all who die in Christ do so? It has been the almost universal belief of Protestants, but there is no Scripture for it. If Solomon's words, "the spirit returns to God who gave it," mean this, then the saints before the time of Christ must have gone there, and, as before remarked, not saints only, but the ungodly also, for the statement applies to all men.

It has been often asserted that when the Lord rose he released from Hades the godly dead and removed them to Paradise in the presence of God, and that ever since all His people go there at death. The Scripture nowhere declares this, but is wholly against it.

It should be asked, *Where* were these multitudes of souls during the forty days before Christ himself ascended? Raised at His resurrection, as the theory asserts, what was their location during that period?

But it is known definitely that one of the most renowned of Old Testament men of God did *not* ascend to heaven with the Lord, for at Pentecost, which was after the ascension, Peter distinctly stated that "David has not ascended into the heavens" (Darby, Acts 2:34). Why was David left behind? There is no reason to think he was: the other godly dead also stayed there, as far as Scripture is concerned.

Alford translates: "David himself [i.e., in contrast to Christ] is not ascended": Whitby: "David is not (yet) ascended": Canon Cook (Speaker's Commentary) remarks: "David's soul was still in the intermediate state." Had David in fact ascended even but a few weeks before Peter was speaking, the latter could not have made the assertion "David ascended not." The aorist used (*anabee*) covered all preceding time, from the death of David to the speech of Peter. Moreover, if at *any* time David had ascended the point and conclusiveness of Peter's argument were gone. Its cogency lay in the fact that *no one* but Jesus Christ had ascended: therefore He and He alone fulfilled the prophecy; for if *anyone* else had ascended from the grave to the throne of God how should it be certain that *he* did not fulfil the prediction?

In his great work on *The Creed* (Art. 5, *He descended into Hell*) Bishop Pearson shows how little basis the opinion in question has. He says: "The next consideration, is whether by virtue of His descent, the souls of those who before believed in Him, the Patriarchs, Prophets, and all the people of God, were delivered from that place and state, in which they were before; and whether Christ *descended into Hell* to that end, that He might translate them into a place and state, far more glorious and happy. This has been, in the later ages of the Church, the vulgar opinion of most men. . . .

"But even this opinion, as general as it hath been, hath neither the consent of Antiquity, nor such certainty as it pretendeth. Indeed, very few (if any) for above five hundred years after Christ, did so believe that Christ delivered the saints out of Hell, as to leave all the damned there. Many of the Ancients believed not, that they were removed at all, and few acknowledged that they were removed alone."

But it is asked, What became of those who came forth from their graves after Christ had risen and who appeared unto many? (Matt. 27:52-53). Did they not "go to heaven" with the Lord? Let those say what became of these to whom God may have given private information upon the point; but it cannot be learned from Scripture that they went to heaven. And in return it may be asked, What became of Lazarus and the other persons who were resuscitated, as mentioned in Scripture? Did they go to heaven without dying again *or*, are they still on earth? *or*, did they not in due time go back to the death state, from which they had been temporarily recalled to exhibit the power of God?

That Christ "led captivity captive" carries no suggestion that He took the godly dead to heaven. The figure itself forbids the idea. It is taken from the ancient practice that a victorious commander dragged many, and the most noble, of his captives to his capital city and exhibited them for his glory at his triumphal entry. The expression could in no wise apply to the possible recovery of some of his own subjects from captivity by his enemy and their return home with him in liberty. The sense may be seen plainly in the place in Judges 5:12, from which the phrase is quoted in the later passages. As the conqueror Barak returns from the victory over Sisera Deborah cries: "Arise, Barak, and lead away thy captives." It is the Lord's conquest of the hosts of darkness that is celebrated in the New Testament passages (Eph. 4:8; Col. 2:15), as it is also the theme in Ps. 68:18, from which the quotation is actually made. The figure is again military. God is pictured as among a mighty host: "The chariots of God are twenty thousand, even thousands upon thousands," and then it is said, "Thou hast led away captives," the phrase formerly used of Barak.

6. When and Where is Paradise?

Paradise is not the actual dwelling place of God, the house or temple in heaven. The meaning of the word will not allow this, for it describes the pleasure grounds of a great man, say a king. Thus Solomon using the word says, "I builded me houses; I planted me vineyards; I made me gardens and parks (paradises, LXX), and I planted trees in them of all kinds of fruits" (Eccl. 2:4-5). The parks were not the houses. The former, like the vineyards, might be at a distance from the palace. In the Septuagint (LXX) the word is used of the garden of Eden.

Paul says that he was "caught away into the paradise" (2 Cor. 12:4), which, in view of the meaning of the word, does not mean the heaven of heavens where God has His own especial dwelling. The word "caught *up*" is not exact, for the Greek word *harpazō* does not in itself indicate the direction. Nor is it certain that by "the paradise" he means the "third heaven" to which he had been taken according to the verse preceding, because he had said (ver. 1) that he was about to speak of "visions," not of only one vision, whereas he did not mention more than one, unless the two are separate events.

But *if* the article "the paradise" points to one such region that is pre-eminently Paradise, and *if* that is in the upper world, what follows? Nothing, as to our theme; certainly not that all saints go thither at death. Paul is using the experience as proof that he had exceptional tokens that he was an apostle, which requires that the experience itself be exceptional, not general. Moreover, that an unusual event happened to one Christian during life is no proof that it happens to all Christians at death.

But the article "the paradise" does not require the sense of a region in the heavens, because Christ used it when he said to the thief, "Today shalt thou be with me in the paradise" (Lk. 23:43), and it is beyond question, as we have seen, that Christ did not go to the heavenly regions that day, but to Hades, in "the lower parts of the earth." Therefore the blissful region of Hades, "Abraham's bosom" (Lk. 16:22) was paradise; and ought not we, the followers of the Lord, to feel that a region which was suitable to Him in the death state must be fully suitable for us?

As far as the meaning of the word goes there may be many paradises, even as Solomon says, "I made me paradises"; and so it may be that "the Paradise of God," where grows the tree of life of which saints that have conquered in the battles of life shall be privileged to eat, is heavenly in location (Rev. 2:7; 22:14); but in any case that is future, not present, as to our enjoyment of it, and does not touch the place and state of the dead.

The Lord Jesus in His universal presence is not only in heaven; He is also in the midst of two or three living saints gathered to His name on earth. He is in Hades also: "He descended ... He ascended, that He might fill all things" might occupy the universe (*ta panta*), might pervade it all with His presence, as the odour of the ointment did the house (John 12:3), where the same verb is used as in Eph. 4:10 (*pleeroō*). Thus, without vacating His place at the right hand of God, He could present Himself personally and repeatedly to His imprisoned and hard-pressed servant on earth (Acts 23:11; 2 Tim. 4:16-17), and can also communicate with the dead, as we shall see shortly.

And the soul, freed from the trammels of this enfeebled, deranged body of our humiliation, can in consequence appreciate that presence more keenly and enjoy it more blessedly, and so Paul could rightly say that to depart and to be with Christ would be very far better than to be chained day and night to a rough pagan soldier, as was at that time his distressing lot (Phil. 1:23). It is however to be noted that the apostle does not here make any general statement that "to die is gain"; strictly his assertion is made of himself only. He had just stated his "earnest expectation and hope" that Christ should continue to be "magnified in his body, whether by life or by death." Not every believer lives with this as his fixed and paramount intention. Not every Christian has so dedicated his body to Christ as to be as willing for death as for life. Then Paul adds: "For *to me* to live is Christ, and to die is gain" (Phil. 1:20-21). Doubtless this is true of each who lives to magnify Christ; but it is not said of believers who may not so live, as those, for example, who are cut off prematurely in their sins, as were Ananias and Sapphira and the evil living Christians in the Corinthian church (Acts 5:1; Cor. 11:30).

7. The Souls Under the Altar

It is a serious loss to many believers that they regard the book of the Revelation as beyond comprehension, and are afraid to accept its symbols and visions as a *revelation*. Hence, when appeal is made to it they decline to accept its testimony. But symbols, pictures, figures of speech, being used by the Spirit of truth with divine care, teach with accuracy, and indeed with superior vividness, those who have eyes to see and ears to hear. Hieroglyphs have plain meaning to those who can read them, and this had been just as much the fact during the period when men could not read them, or in the later period when scholars differed as to their meaning. Patient research brought explanation and reconciliation.

One of the most illuminating portions of Scripture upon our present interesting and necessary themes is in Revelation 6:9-11. John says: "And when the Lamb opened the fifth seal, I saw underneath the altar the souls of them that had been slain for the word of God, and for the testimony which they held: and they cried with a great voice, saying, How long, O sovereign ruler, the holy and true, dost thou not judge and avenge our blood on them that dwell on the earth? And there was given to them, to each one, a white robe; and it was said unto them that they should rest yet for a little time, until their fellow-bondmen also and their brethren, who should be killed even as they were, should have fulfilled their course."

At the time here in view the resurrection of the godly has not yet come, for the roll of the martyrs is not complete. These brethren therefore are still without their resurrection bodies. But to John, rapt in spirit into that super-sensuous world (c. 1:10: "I became in spirit," that is, in an ecstatic state), those "souls" were visible. Therefore death does not end the existence of the *soul*. Moreover, they are conscious: they remember what befell them on earth at the hands of the godless; they know what the future will bring of vengeance; they ponder the situation, and they wonder at the seeming delay of their vindication by God; they appeal to their Lord; they are given answer, counsel, and encouragement; they receive the sign of their Master's approval, the white robe, at once His recompense for that they did not defile their garments in this foul world, and His assurance that they shall be His personal and constant associates in His kingdom (Rev. 3:4-5). This last item—the giving of the white robes—shows further that not all saints await a session of the judgment seat of Christ when at last He shall come from heaven; for His decision and approval are here made known to these in advance of His coming and of their resurrection.

The vision contains also something more, and which is completely unseen by most readers.

When Samuel came from Hades to speak to Saul (1 Sam. 28:12-14) he was *seen* by the medium. She saw him "coming up out of the earth," a further plain intimation that Sheol is within the earth. She described him, saying it was "an old man" who had appeared, and he was "covered with a robe." The description was so accurate that Saul, who had long known Samuel on earth, recognized him by it and was satisfied that the real Samuel was present, though he had not himself seen the appearance; for it says that "he perceived (Heb., knew)," not that he *saw* that it was Samuel. Equally does his question to the witch "What seest *thou*?" tell that he had not himself seen the form.

This makes evident (a) that the disembodied soul has form and garments, such as can be seen by one endowed with vision therefor, as were the medium then and John later; and (b) that the psychical form and clothing of that state correspond recognizably to the outer material form and clothing of the former earth life. This has bearing upon the question of recognition after death, and upon other interesting points not now to be examined.

The reality of this psychical form is often assumed or asserted in Scripture. Dives in Hades (Lk. 16) has a body that can feel anguish from a "flame." There is "water" that could cool his "tongue." Lazarus has a "finger." Both Dives and Abraham have eyes and ears and voices; they see and hear and speak. The reality of bliss in that state must be surrendered if the reality of torment there be denied. That those realities are subtle as compared with their grosser counterparts of this world, does not make them or the experiences less real, but rather the more acute.

Thus also it is as to the souls "under the altar." John sees them, and sees that to each of them is given a "robe" that is both suitable and significant.

It was for a similar, yet even higher, experience that Paul longed; for, while the disembodied state would indeed be far better than his painful lot as a prisoner, yet in itself it is not the best. And so on another occasion, when he was in freedom and rejoicing in his wondrous and privileged service, he spoke differently (2 Cor. 5:1-10). First he spoke of the present: "We that are in this tent-dwelling [the body] do groan, being burdened": then he mentioned the intermediate state after death: "not for that we would be unclothed" (without adequate covering), for this is not to be desired, it is as unpleasant and unseemly for the soul as for the body[1]; and then he spoke of the future: "we long to be clothed upon with our habitation which

---

1. Compare the evident longing of the evil spirit to return into the body he had left. Without a material body he wandered restless, like a thirsty man seeking water in a desert (Matt. 12:43-45). Demons also begged to enter the bodies of even swine, when driven from the body of a man. This misery of disembodied beings is recognized by the heathen, who often, by reason of dread and unholy contact with the demon world, have more sense of these matters than the materialized modern westerner. Thus a Chinese driver explained the whirling dust spouts of the Gobi desert as being spirits: "What they want is a body, and for lack of a better one they pick up a shroud of sand" (Misses Cable and French, *Something Happened*, 191).

is from heaven; if so be that being clothed we shall not be found naked," that is, at the coming of the Lord.

This "if so be" implies the possibility of not having part in the first resurrection, for (1 Cor. 15:54) that is the hour when "what is mortal shall be swallowed up of life," by the soul being clothed upon with its "building from God, a house not made with hands, eternal, in the heavens," a "house" in contrast to this present body, the frail transitory tent.

This is the meaning of his earlier prayer above noticed, that "the spirit and soul and body be preserved *entire,* unblemished," and so unblamable (*amemptōs* includes both) when the Lord shall come (1 Thess. 5:22). No "naked," that is, unembodied, soul can be presented before the presence of God's glory, because for that it must be without blemish (*amomōs*), not to be blamed (Jude 24; Eph. 1:4). Were a man, however perfect his form, and even were he of the royal family, to present himself naked on a court day before the king upon his throne he would be severely blamed. Not only comeliness of person, but clothing, and suitable clothing, is indispensable. Indeed, the officers of the court would prevent anything so utterly unseemly. Shall the King of kings receive less respect? He that hath ears to hear let him hear this, and lay to heart that not death, but resurrection or rapture fits for translation to the realms above and the court of the God of glory. It was thus with Christ himself.

For entrance into the holy places the priest had not only to be one of the redeemed people of God; he had also to be unblemished as to his person (Lev. 21), and he had further to be clothed in garments of glory and beauty (Ex. 28). Both were indispensable for access to the presence of God. Moreover, before the perfect form could be clothed in such garments it had to be washed with water (Lev. 8:6; 16:4), which is the work our Moses, Christ, wishes to effect in us in this earthly life by His word (Eph. 5:25-27) and by discipline (Heb. 12:10), in preparation for that coming day of our being clothed for access to and service in the true sanctuary above.

If it be asked whether the righteousness imputed to the believer upon first faith in Christ does not include all this that is evidently necessary, the answer is a distinct negative. One consideration settles this. That imputed righteousness is the "righteousness of God," and this is of necessity indefectible, untarnishable. But, according to the regulations, the priest may possibly be defective in form or defiled in person and clothing: were it not so, what need of the regulations and purifying ceremonies?

For the forgiveness of sins, and for life as a forgiven man *in the camp,* neither perfection of form, nor washing at the gate of the tabernacle, nor special clothing, were demanded; but for access to God and for priestly service all these were as indispensable as the atoning blood. Imputed righteousness settles completely and for ever the judicial standing of the believer as justified before the law of God; but practical righteousness must be added in order to secure many of the mighty privileges which become possible to the justified. Let him that hath ears hear this also, for loss and shame must be his at last who has been content to remain deformed and imperfect in moral state, or is found to have neglected the washing, and so to be unfit to wear the noble clothing required for access to the throne of glory. Such neglect of present grace not only causes the loss of heart access to God, as the careless believer surely knows, but will assure the forfeiture of much that grace would have granted in the future.

Here lies the weight of the warning which our Lord announces from heaven as to be specially applicable when His coming draws near: "Behold, I come as a thief. [This message is set in the midst of the gathering of the hosts of Antichrist for the battle of Har Magedon, and so indicates the period when the coming will be]. Blessed is he that watcheth, and keepeth his garments, lest he walk naked and they see his shame" (Rev. 16:15). Therefore "garments" may be lost. If the reference is to the imputed righteousness, then justification may be forfeited, and the once saved be afterwards lost. But let those who rightly reject this, inquire honestly what it does properly mean as to the eternally justified. And let them face what is involved in the loss of one's garments.

In the temple of old the guards were placed at nightfall at their posts. The captain of the temple, at any hour he chose, went round with a posse of men unannounced, and if a guard was caught asleep at his post, he was stripped of his clothes, which were burned, and he was left to go forth in his shame. The shame of his nakedness was the outward counterpart of the deeper shame that he had slept when on duty. Not in that dishonoured state dare he enter the house of God and sing or serve. And it would be long ere the disgrace of that night would fade from memory, his own or others. My soul, keep awake through this short night of duty while thy Lord is away! Thou knowest not in which watch of the night He will come, and it were dreadful to be left unclothed with that house which is from heaven should He come suddenly and find thee sleeping!

To return to seal 5. These, then, are "souls" not "spirits." Man has spirit as part of his composite being, but he is not a spirit, as angels are. In the 397 places where the word "spirit" comes in the New Testament man is never called a spirit, because he *himself* is not one, but is a *soul*. Hence, by the way, the "in-prison spirits" of 1 Pet. 3:19 are not human beings, but those fallen angels whom Peter again mentions (2 Pet. 2:4: comp. Gen. 6:1-4 and Jude 6). This is put beyond question by the fact that these are in the underworld, in prison, in Tartarus—a region well known to the ancient world, and by this name that Peter uses, as the deepest and most dreadful part of Hades, a prison of fallen angels; whereas the *spirit* of *man* does not go to the underworld, but to "God who gave it."

It is therefore the soul which is the person; and—against the annihilationist—the soul has not ceased to exist, or lost its sense of personality, because of being without spirit or body. Yet neither can man in this incomplete condition stand in the all-holy presence of God in heaven. For entrance into the holy of holies the high priest himself must be arrayed in garments specially pure and glorious. It was only in His resurrection body of glory that the Man Christ Jesus entered into the holy place on high, and so only can the under-priests, His followers, do so. To stand there the being must be complete in structure and perfect morally, which is the point of Paul's prayer for fellow-saints: "The God of peace himself *sanctify* you *wholly;* and may your spirit and soul and body be preserved entire, blameless in the parousia [the presence, at His coming] of our Lord Jesus Christ" (1 Thess. 5:23). This shows that the phrase "the spirits of just men made perfect" points to the resurrection. It has just before been said of them, that "apart from us they could not be made perfect" (Heb. 12:23; 11:40). All the other glories to which in this passage we are said to have come are future, to be realized actually at the coming of the Lord. See my *Firstborn Sons,* 84 ff.

The use of *spirit* in this place (Heb. 12:23) may *seem* at variance with the statement that man is not called a "*spirit!*" It is a rare instance, perhaps in the New Testament the only instance, of Cremer's fourth sense in which the term is used. It "comes to denote an essence without any corporeal garb for its inner reality"; that is, in Heb. 12:23, which he cites, the man, the soul, without its body, is described as *spirit,* meaning a spiritual substance destitute of a material covering. This does not cancel the regular distinction in Scripture between *soul* and *spirit,* but indicates only the immateriality of the soul, the ego, in itself. The student should by all means study Cremer's treatment of *pneuma* and *psuchē* (*Lexicon of N.T. Greek*), and note his conclusion that "*psuchē* [soul] is the subject or *ego* of life."

Now these souls that John saw are "under the altar." Not one of the first six seals, of which this is the fifth, pictures events in the presence of God in heaven; all deal with affairs of earth, or as seen from the earth. This altar, then, is not in heaven. There is an altar in heaven pictured in the book, but it is specified as being the "golden altar," that is, the one for incense (comp. Ex. 30:3), and as being "before the throne" or "before God" (Rev. 8. 3; 9:13). In this book "before the throne" always means the upper heavens. But this other altar is one of sacrifice, though not of atoning sacrifice. We Christians have an altar of atoning sacrifice (Heb. 13:10): it is the cross of Jesus, the Lamb of God. But that is not in view here.

The picture is really quite simple. The brazen altar of sacrifice in the tabernacle was square and hollow, with a grating upon which rested the wood and the victims. When the fire had done its work the remains of the sacrifice fell through the grating to beneath the altar, whence they could be removed on occasion. Now the place, the "altar," where these martyrs of Christ sacrificed person and life in His cause is obviously this earth, and thus this vision simply declares what we have seen from other scriptures, that the place of the dead is under the earth: "He descended into the lower parts of the earth"; whence those still there will be removed at resurrection.

Since these pages were written I have learned that this was the explanation of the earliest known Latin commentator on the Apocalypse, Victorinus of Pettau (died 303). Mr. F. F. Bruce summarized this in *The Evangelical Quarterly* (Oct., 1938) as follows: "The altar (6:9) is the earth: the brazen altar of burnt-offering and the golden altar of incense in the Tabernacle correspond to earth and heaven respectively. *The souls under the altar,* therefore, are in Hades, in that department of it which is 'remote from pains and fires, the rest of the saints'."

This confirms Bishop Pearson cited above as to the view held in the earliest Christian centuries.

A great deal more concerning Hades can be learned from Scripture, but it would require separate treatment. Here we deal with the matter only as connected with the subject in hand.

It is true, as above indicated on Heb. 12:23, that the words soul and spirit take, by much usage, shades of meaning derived from their primary sense. The student will discover these, and will not be confused thereby if only the primary, dominant sense of each has been first grasped firmly. And keeping that sense before him, we believe he will find it to illuminate many obscure scriptures and subjects to see that the *soul* is the person—a living soul while on earth—a dead soul while in the underworld—and to be made alive in immortality at the resurrection, with a body of glory incorruptible, indestructible.

The term "immortal soul" is incorrect and misleading when used of our present state or of the dead. To be immortal is to be incapable of dying. Man is not this as yet. Neither the innocent humanity of Adam, nor even the sinless humanity of Jesus was immortal, for both were capable of dying, and did in fact die. But the saved of men will become immortal in resurrection, as the man Christ Jesus did. The soul, the man, has now *endless existence* but not immortality, in the proper sense of the word, until resurrection; and then only the saved will be incapable of dying; the lost will exist for ever, but in a state termed "dead," the "second death."

We rightly describe death as a "dissolution," for the partnership between man's spirit and soul and body is dissolved. Of our Lord in resurrection we read the glorious fact that "He liveth in the power of *indissoluble* life" and "death no more hath dominion over Him" (Heb. 7:16; Rom. 6:9-10). This life His people will share for ever and ever. But for them, as for Him, it can be reached only by resurrection or rapture, never by death. It will be no small profit from this discussion if it be seen that the opinion that the believer goes at death to glory diminishes the sense of need of resurrection or rapture, and consequently of the return of Christ when these will take place; and also if it thus cause some hearts to feel that these events are utterly indispensable, the proper, the blessed hope of the believer. As Peter exhorts, let us "set our hope perfectly [that is, undividedly] on the favour that is being brought unto us at the revelation of Jesus Christ" (1 Pet. 1:13).

6
The Judgment Seat of Christ

1. God has an inescapable duty to be the "Judge of all the earth" (Gen. 18:25). Those who submit to Him are subject to this judgment equally with the insubordinate: "The Lord shall judge *His people*" (Deut. 32:36; Ps. 135:14; Heb. 10:30). The children of the sovereign are amenable to the laws and the courts and liable to penalty for misconduct.

2. This judgment is ever in process. There is a perpetual overruling of human affairs by higher authorities. Prominent instances are Job (ch. 1 and 2), Ahab (1 Kin. 22), Nebuchadnezzar (Dan. 4). The first case shows the judicial proceedings effecting perfecting, the second death, the third reformation.

Job was a godly man under discipline for his good: an upright man was made a holy man. Thus still does God chasten His sons that they may become partakers of His holiness (Heb. 12:10-11).

Sinning Christians were disciplined even unto premature death, and it is explained that this operates to save them from liability to condemnation at the time when God will deal with the world at large (1 Cor. 11:32).

3. But this continuous judicial administration has its crisis sessions, its special occasions. Instances are: the Flood; the destruction of Sodom and Gomorrah; the judgments on Egypt at the time of the exodus of Israel; the destruction of the seven nations of Canaan by Israel; the overthrow of Jerusalem by Nebuchadnezzar; and later by Titus.

Hereafter there will come the destruction of Gentile world dominion and the punishment of Antichrist. Then the judgment at Jerusalem of the living (Joel 2; Matt. 25), when the Lord has returned to Zion. And after the thousand years the final session of the court of God, the great white throne, whereat will be declared the eternal destiny of those there judged.

But it is most necessary to keep in mind that all such separate and specific sessions are but part of the ceaselessly operating judicial administration of heaven and earth.

4. It is important to remember that the Son of man is the chief Judge of the universe. It was He who acted at the Flood: "Jehovah sat as king at the Flood" (Ps. 29:10). It was He who, in holy care that only justice should be done, came down to enquire personally whether Sodom and Gomorrah ought to be destroyed (Gen. 18:20-21), and Who again came down to deliver Israel from Egypt (Ex. 3:7-8). It was His glory as judge that was seen by Isaiah (ch. 6; John 12:41), and later by Ezekiel (ch. 1).

He is the Man appointed to judge the world in righteousness on behalf of God the Father (Acts 17:31); for the Father has entrusted all judgment unto the Son, in order that He may receive equal honour with the Father (John 5:19-29).

5. Yet it is particularly needful to note that the last cited passage is in reference to the *future* sessions of the divine judgment, for the judging in question is there set in direct connection with the raising of men from the dead (John 5:21-22, 27-29). For when the Son of God became man He ceased for the present to supervise those judgments of heaven. This was among the dignities of which He emptied, that is, divested Himself, for His immediate and blessed purpose in becoming man was their salvation from judgment (John 5:24). Therefore He said: "God sent not the Son into the world to judge the world, but that the world should be saved through Him" (John 3:17); nor has He yet resumed the office of supreme Judge, though appointed thereto as man. In relation to the world He is still the Dispenser of the grace of God, not yet the Executor of His holy wrath, as He will one day become.

This is clear from three chief considerations:

(i) That the Father has called Him to sit at His own right hand until the time when His enemies are to be put under His feet (Ps. 110:1; Heb. 1:13; 10:13). That is, He is not yet sitting upon His own throne and asserting His own right and authority, as He will do in a later day (Rev. 2:26-27; 3:21: Matt. 25:31); but He is waiting expectantly that coming day.

(ii) And therefore is it twice pictured that, as Son of man, the Lamb, He is hereafter to be brought before the Father to be invested officially with that authority to judge and to make war the title to which is His already but the exercise of which is in abeyance (Dan. 7:13-14; Rev. ch. 4 and 5). In both of these scenes it is God the Father who is shown acting from the throne of judgment until the Son has been thus formally installed as Judge.

(iii) And therefore is He now the Advocate of His people before the Father (1 John 2:1). But the Advocate cannot be at the same time the Judge.

6. Thus during this interval the especial concern and sphere of the Son of man is the company He is calling out of the world, the church of God. The building of His church is His present work (Matt. 16:18): the regulating of the affairs of the house of God, over which He as Son is the appointed ruler (Heb. 3:6), is His immediate and dear concern.

And this work calls for both grace and judgment. He "can bear gently with the ignorant and the erring, sympathizing with our infirmities" (Heb. 5:2; 4:15), but dealing with kind severity with the wilful of His people. "Behold then the goodness and severity of God" (Rom. 11:22). Nor may we abuse His goodness by making light of His severity; or if we do, it will be unto painful disillusionment.

7. Judgment upon His own people therefore God exercises now; this is the very period for it; but the general judgment of the world is deferred: "The time is come for judgment to begin at the house of God" (1 Pet. 4:17). And again: "If we discriminated [sat in strict judgment upon] ourselves, we should not be judged, but when [failing in this holy self-judgment] we are judged, we are chastened by the Lord [here perhaps the Father, comp. Heb. 12:5, 9, where He who chastens is the Father of spirits] that we may not be condemned with the world" (1 Cor. 11:30-31). And this chastening may extend to bodily weakness, positive sickness, or even death. So it was in the cases of Ananias and Sapphira (Acts 5:1-11, and see Jas. 5:19-20; 1 John 5:16-17; Matt. 5:21-26; 18:28-35).

8. The Lord made many most serious statements as to His dealings with "His own" servants at His return. Some of these are:

(i) Luke 12:22-53. From dealing with the crowd He turns and speaks specifically to His own disciples (ver. 22). Only genuine disciples, regenerated persons, are able to fulfil His precepts here given. To mere professors the task is impossible, and such cannot be in view. They are to live without any anxiety as to the necessities of life, and in this are to be in express contrast to the nations; they are His "little flock," for whom the Father intends the kingdom, and therefore they are to give away, not to hoard, and so to lay up treasure in heaven (21-34). It is impossible to include the unregenerate in such a passage; nor would it be attempted save to avoid the application to Christians of part of the succeeding and connected instruction.

This instruction is that disciples are like the personal household slaves of an absent master, who upon his return will deal with each according to his conduct during the master's absence. In particular, the steward set over the household will be dealt with the more strictly that his office, opportunities, and example were the higher. The goodness of the master is seen in exalting the faithful (though from one point of view he had done no more than his duty and was an unprofitable servant) to almost unlimited privilege and power: "He will set him over all that he hath" (ver. 44): his severity is shown by "cutting in sunder"[1] the servant who had abused his trust, and appointing his portion with the unfaithful (35-53).

(ii) This is elaborated and enforced in later statements. Luke 19: 11-27. The picture is the same, namely, the absent master and the faithful or unfaithful servants. The "pound" represents that deposit of truth entrusted to the saints (Jude 3), for their use among men while Christ is away: "Trade ye till I come." The Nobleman himself held and used it while here, and left it with us when He went to receive the kingdom. If we traffic with knowledge it increases in our hands and we gain more; if we neglect to do so it remains truth, retaining its own intrinsic value ("thou hast thy pound"), but we do not accumulate knowledge, nor benefit others, nor bring to our Lord any return for His confidence in us. In this parable it is not the personal life of the slave that is in question; that may have been good: it is

---

1. Equals "severely scourge," because the scourge used cut deeply into the flesh—see margin.

The Judgment Seat of Christ

his use of the truth in either spreading it among man, or hiding his light under a bushel of silence, or, as the picture is here, burying the pound in the earth.

The unfaithful servant loses opportunity further to serve his lord, the pound is taken from him. Sadder still, his lord has no confidence in him. But he is not an *enemy* of his lord, nor is treated as such. He does not lose his life. The contrast is most distinct between him, however unfaithful, and the foes and rebels: "*But* these mine enemies that would not that I should reign over them, bring hither and slay them before me" (ver. 27).

(iii) Matt. 24:42-25:30. Only a few days later the Lord repeated this instruction, with fuller detail. The head slave, set as steward of the house during the absence of the master, will be set over all his lord's possessions if only he have acted faithfully (45-47). "But if *that* evil servant" abuses his position, and becomes self-indulgent and tyrannical, he will be "severely scourged," and his portion be allotted with the hypocrites, where he will weep and gnash his teeth over his folly and lot.

Only a believer who does not consider his own heart will assert that a Christian cannot act the hypocrite, be unfaithful, or arbitrary and unloving. But the pronoun "that"—"But if *that* evil servant, etc.," leaves no option but to regard him as a believer, for it has no antecedent to whom it can refer except the faithful servant just before described, no other person having been mentioned. "*That* evil servant"; *what* evil servant? and there is no answer but that the faithful steward has become unfaithful[2]: *And such cases are known*. Nor will we, for our part, join to consign all such to *eternal* ruin rather than accept the alternative of the temporary, though severe, punishments intimated by the Lord being possible to a believer. Those who take the latter course, mainly influenced to support certain dispensational theories, have surely never weighed the solemnity of thus easily consigning so many backsliders to endless misery.

Since, then, an unbeliever is (a) not set by *the Lord* over His house, nor (b) could feed the souls of his fellows, nor (c) could be so

---

2. Weymouth is definite: "But if that man, being a bad servant" plainly identifies the good and bad servant as one person. And see Alford.

faithful as to become at last ruler of all the possessions of the Lord, this man must be a true believer. But when such a one may lapse from his fidelity he does not thereby become unregenerate; consequently the unfaithful steward is still called one of the Lord's "own servants"; and therefore a believer may incur the solemn penalties veiled under the figures used.

If it be thought inconceivable that the Lord should describe one of His blood-bought and beloved people as a "wicked servant" (Matt. 25:26), it must be weighed that He had before applied the term to a servant whose "debt" had been fully remitted: "thou wicked servant, I forgave thee all that debt" (Matt. 18:32). Thus one who, as an act of compassion by the Lord, has been fully forgiven all his failure as a servant may prove a "wicked servant," his wickedness consisting in this, that though forgiven he would not forgive. To deny that a child of God can be unforgiving is to blind the eyes by denying sad and stem fact. The Lord left no room for doubt that members of the divine family were in His mind by the application of the parable He then and there made: "Even so shall my heavenly *Father* do unto *you* [Peter, whose question as to forgiving had drawn forth the parable, and the other disciples, ver. 1, 21], if ye forgive not, each one of you (*hekastos*), his *brother* from your hearts" (35). It is the *Father* and the *brothers* who are in question, not here those outside the family circle.

Moreover, if this parable be pressed to include a mere professing but unregenerate person some inevitable implications must be accepted. It is by no means denied that there are such persons, but if they are in view here these consequences follow:

(a) An unregenerate person has had "all his debt forgiven."

(b) In spite of this free forgiveness he *remains unregenerate.*

(c) A forgiven sinner can have the free pardon of his sins revoked, in which case he will thereafter stand in his former lost estate exposed to the eternal wrath of God. He may be saved today yet lose this tomorrow.

(d) Though delivered to the "tormentors" he may entertain hope that he may yet himself "pay all that is due" (ver. 34); that is, the wrath of God against the unregenerate can be somehow, some time satisfied by the sufferings and efforts of *the sinner himself.* In these

The Judgment Seat of Christ

cases therefore "Christ died for nought"; they can at last secure their own deliverance.

In the fact, however, being "delivered to the tormentors" has no reference to the eternal judgment of the lost. In the lake of fire neither lost angels nor lost men are stated to torment one another, but are all alike in the same torment. It is a picture of present and temporal chastisement under that continually proceeding judgment of God above indicated, and which applies to His family as to others. Regarded thus the above confusing implications do not arise, implications which no one divinely illuminated could accept. But it results that the wicked servant is a real servant, not a hypocrite, and were it not for the severity of the punishment no one would be likely to question this.

It is not difficult to see what the punishment is.

(a) The forgiveness of his great failures *as a servant* can be revoked, and he be made to feel the sin and bitterness of not having walked by the same spirit as his Lord, nor rendered to Him the due use and return of the benefits grace had bestowed.

(b) Paul says of some who had once had faith and a good conscience (or they could not have thrust these away), and who had started on the voyage of faith (or they could not have made shipwreck), "whom I delivered to Satan" (the present "tormentor," as of Job); but not to be afflicted by him in hell, but for their recovery, "that they might be taught not to blaspheme," which the torments of the damned will not teach *them,* as far as we see in the Word (1 Tim. 1:19-20. See also 1 Cor. 5:3-5).

(iv) We remark upon one other instance of these solemn testimonies by Christ, the parable of the virgins (Matt. 25). It is to the same effect.

(a) They are all *virgins,* the foolish equally with the wise, which figure is inappropriate to indicate a worldling in his sins, even though he be a professing Christian. In the only other places where it is used figuratively and spiritually it certainly means true Christians (2 Cor. 11:2; Rev. 14:4).

(b) They are all equally the invited guests of the bridegroom, not strangers, let alone his enemies.

(c) They *all* have oil, or, the foolish could not say "our lamps are *going* out." Without some oil the lamps could not even have been lit, for a dry wick will not kindle and certainly could not have burned during the time they had slept.

(d) But the foolish had no supply to replenish the dimly burning flax and revive their testimony. They had formerly been "light in the Lord," but had been thoughtless as to grace to continue alight.

(e) They found means for this renewing for in spite of the darkness they gained the bridegroom's gate.

(f) They did not lose their lives, as enemies, but they did lose the marriage feast, and were left in the darkness outside the house. This is parallel to the "wicked servant," who also did not lose his life but did lose the entrance into the joy of his master at his return, and was cast into "outer darkness."

Two observations are vital to grasping the meaning of these judgments.

(i) A marriage feast is obviously no picture of anything eternal. Plainly it is a temporary matter. Grand, intensely happy, a highly coveted honour, especially when the king's son, the heir apparent, is the bridegroom, it yet is but the *prelude* to a life, a reign, not anything long-extended, let alone permanent. Does not this correspond to the joy of the millennial kingdom as the glorious prelude to the eternal kingdom? For the "marriage of the Lamb" comes at the immediate inception of that millennial kingdom (Rev. 19:6-9). And are not the invited virgins those of whom verse 9 says, "Blessed are they that are bidden to the marriage supper of the Lamb," rather than the wife herself? A bride is not usually invited to her wedding feast: it cannot (save, perhaps, among Moslems) be held without her. Does not this give the clue to what the virgins and the unfaithful servant lose?

(ii) "Outer darkness" is no picture of the lake of fire. It is the realm just outside the palace where the feast is held, not the public prison or execution ground. If the strict sense of Scripture pictures be kept, and imagination be not allowed to fill in what the Divine Artist did not put in, much confusion will be avoided.

It has been felt that the words of the bridegroom to the virgins, "Verily I say unto you, I know you not" preclude us from taking these

The Judgment Seat of Christ

to represent His true people. But again the picture itself will give the real sense. The bridegroom is here pictured as standing within the heavy and thick outer door that secures every eastern house of quality, and the door is shut. He does not open it, or he would see who they are, and that they are some of his own invited guests, but standing the other side of the closed door he says, in idiomatic English, *I tell you sincerely, I don't know who you are (Ameen legō humin, ouk oida humas)*. Into such a picture it is not permissible to read in divine omniscience; it must be taken simply as it is given.

Its force may be gathered more readily by the distinction between what is here said and what the Lord said in Matt. 7:15-23. There He spoke of false prophets, bad trees, men who, like the sons of Sceva in Acts 19:13, used His holy name without warrant. Picturing Himself as standing face to face with these He protests, *I never at any time made your acquaintance!* Here the scene is changed; there is no closed door between: the verb to know is different: and the word rendered "never" is most emphatic and gives force and finality to the assertion (*Oudepote egnōn humas*). He did not speak thus to the virgins.

9. It is not our present purpose to consider all such testimony of the Word. Enough has been advanced to show how much and how solemn is the teaching of Scripture as to judgment upon careless Christians. We wish only to deal now with the *time* of the judgment seat of Christ as to His people.

The most general opinion is that this judgment lies between the moment of the Lord's descent to the air, when they, dead and living, are caught up to Him there, and that later moment when He is to descend with them to the earth to set up His kingdom. That is, the judging of His saints will take place during the Parousia.

Observations.

(i) No passage of Scripture seems distinctly to place this judgment in this interval and in the air. It seems to be rather assumed that it must take place then and there since the effects of it are to be seen in the different positions and honours in the kingdom immediately to follow.

(ii) As regards the parabolic instruction Christ gave when here it is to be observed that it speaks only of persons who will be found alive when the "nobleman," "the master of the house" returns. Strictly, therefore, these parables tell nothing as to the time and circumstances of the judgment of dead believers. It must be allowed that the principles of justice will be the same for dead and living, but the details as to the judgment of the former cannot be learned from these passages.

(iii) Some presuppositions held are:

(a) That every believer will share in the first resurrection and the millennial kingdom.

(b) The opposite, that not every believer will do so.

(c) That the judgment of the Lord will result in some of His people suffering loss of reward because of unfaithfulness, but nothing more than loss. This involves that none of the positive and painful inflictions denounced can affect true believers.

(d) The opposite, that the regenerate may incur positive chastisement as a consequence of the Lord's judgment at that time. Thus in *Touching the Coming of the Lord* (84, 85. ed. 1), upon Col. 3:25, "For he that doeth wrong shall receive again the wrong that he hath done (margin): and there is no respect of persons," Hogg and Vine apply this text to that judgment of Christ at His parousia, and say: "It may be difficult for us to conceive how God will fulfil this word to those who are already in bodies of glory, partakers of the joy of the redeemed in salvation consummated in spirit, soul and body. Yet may we be assured that the operation of this law is not to be suspended even in their case. He that 'knoweth how to deliver the godly out of temptation, and to keep the unrighteous under punishment unto the day of judgment' (2 Pet. 2:9), knows also how to direct and to use the working of His law of sowing and reaping in the case of His children also. The attempt to alleviate the text of some of its weight by suggesting that the law operates only in this life, fails, for there is nothing in the text or context to lead the reader to think other than that while the sowing is here the reaping is hereafter. It is clear that if it were not for this supposed difficulty of referring the words to the Christian in the condition in which, as we know from other Scriptures, he will appear at the Judgment seat of Christ, the question whether that time and place were intended would not be raised."

(e) Some (Govett, Pember, and others) who hold that the millennial kingdom may be forfeited by gross sin, suppose that all believers rise in the first resurrection, appear before the judgment-seat of Christ, and being adjudged by Him unworthy of the kingdom they return to the death state to await the second resurrection and the great white throne judgment. Their names being then as believers found in the book of life, they have eternal life in the eternal kingdom, but they will have missed the honour of sharing in and reigning in the millennial age.

These two last ideas (d) and (e) seem alike utterly impossible. It seems wholly inconceivable that a body heavenly, spiritual, glorified, like indeed to the body of the Son of God himself, can be subjected to chastisement for guilt incurred by misuse of the present sin-marred body. Not only the manner of the infliction but the fact of it seems to us out of the question.

It seems equally so that a body that is immortal and incorruptible can admit of its owner passing again into the death state. The ideas and the terms are mutually contradictory and exclusive. Of those who rise in that first resurrection the Lord said plainly: "neither can they die any more" (Lk. 20:36).

What, then, is the solution of these difficulties?

10. We turn to passages dealing directly with the subject.

(i) 2 Cor. 5:10. "We make it our aim, whether at home or absent, to be well-pleasing unto Him. For we must all be made manifest before the judgment-seat of Christ; that each one may receive the things done through the body, according to what he hath done, whether it be good or bad." This chief statement leaves unmentioned the time and place of the judgment.

(ii) Heb. 9:27. "It is laid up for men once to die and after this judgment" (*meta de touto krisis,* no article). Thus judgment may take place at any time after death. Luke 16 shows Dives suffering anguish immediately after death, for the scene is Hades, the realm of the dead between death and resurrection, and his brothers are still alive on earth. But again, Rev. 20:11-15, shows another, the final judgment, after resurrection, after the millennial kingdom. Both are "after death."

Neither of these passages suggests the *parousia* in the air as the time or place.

(iii) The statements of the Lord as to His dealing with His own servants at His return, contemplate that His enemies will be called before Him immediately after He will have dealt with His own household: "But these mine enemies, who would not that I should reign over them, bring hither, and slay them before me" (Lk. 19:27). "Hither," that is, to the same spot where He had just been dealing with His servants. This, as to servants then alive on earth at least, excludes the parousia in the air, for His enemies will not be gathered there.

(iv) Luke 16:19-31. Dives and Lazarus are seen directly after death in conditions the exact reverse of those just before known on earth. The passing of the soul to that other world, and the bringing about of so thorough a change of condition, is too striking, too solemn just *to happen*. Someone must have decided and ordered this reversal; that is, there must have been a judging of their cases and a judicial decision as to what should be their lot in the intermediate state.

This judgment therefore may take place at or immediately after death, as Heb. 9:27 above. And in the time of Christ thus almost all men believed. See, for example, the judgment of Ani directly after death, before Osiris the god of the underworld, in the Egyptian *Book of the Dead*. Or, as to the Pharisees, to whom particularly Christ spoke of Dives and Lazarus, see Josephus, *Antiquities*, 18:3.

(v) 2 Tim. 4:6, 7, 8. "I am already being poured out as a drink offering, and the time of my departure is come. I have fought the good fight, I have kept the faith; I have finished the course, henceforth there is laid up for me the crown of righteousness, which the Lord, the righteous judge, shall give to me at that day: and not only to me, but also to all them that have loved His appearing."

Paul was now certain he had won his crown. When writing to the Philippians a few years before (3:10-14) he spoke uncertainly: "not that I have already obtained," for then he had not yet finished the course; but now he writes with certainty. How could this assurance have become his save by communication from the Righteous Judge?

But this implies that the Judge had both formed and communicated His decision upon Paul's life and service, even though Paul had not yet actually died. In such a case, as it would seem, any session of the judgment seat "in that day" will be only for bestowment of the crown already won and allotted, not for adjudication upon the race or contest, the latter having before taken place as to such a person.

(vi) The expression "I have finished my course" is taken from the athletic world which held so large a place in Greek life and interest and is so often used by Paul as a picture of spiritual effort. In 1 Cor. 9:24-27, it is used as a plain warning that the coveted prize may be lost. Phil. 3:12-14 employs it to urge to intense and unremitting effort to win that prize. The Lord is the righteous Judge, sitting to adjudicate upon each contestant in the race or contest.

Now of unavoidable necessity the judge of the games automatically formed his decision as to each racer or wrestler as each finished the course or the contest. The giving of the prizes was indeed deferred to the close of the whole series of events: Paul's crown would be actually given "in that day"; but not till then did the judge defer his decision as to each item or contestant. It could not be, for the most celebrated of the Greek games, the Olympic, lasted five days.

The figure, taken with the case of Paul, and in the light of Dives and Lazarus, suggests a decision of the Lord as to each believer before or at the time of his death. That decision issues in determining the place and experience of the man in the intermediate state, and may extend to assurance that he has won the crown, the prize of the high calling.

(vii) Rev. 6:9, 11. The Fifth Seal. As before shown, these martyrs "under the altar" are not yet raised from the dead, for others have yet to be killed for Christ's sake, and only then will they be all vindicated and avenged. But to each one of them separately a white robe is given. Now ch. 3:4, 5, shows that the white robe is the visible sign, conferred by the Lord, of their worthiness to be His companions in His glory and kingdom. This again makes evident that for these the Lord's judgment has been formed and announced. No later adjudication upon such is needful or conceivable: only the giving of the crown "in that day."

11. From these facts and considerations it seems fairly clear that the judgment of the Lord upon the dead of His people is not deferred to one session but is reached and declared either (a) immediately before death (as Paul), when there is no further risk of the racer failing, or (b) immediately after death (as Lazarus), or (c) at least in the intermediate state of death (the souls under the altar).

If this is so, then it will follow that the decision of the Lord as to whether a believer is worthy of the first resurrection and reigning in the kingdom is reached prior to resurrection, in which case the two insoluble problems above stated simply do not arise; that is, there is no question of one raised in a deathless state returning to the death state, nor of bodies of glory being subjected to chastisement. Believers adjudged not worthy of the first resurrection will not rise, but will remain where they are until the second resurrection.

We agree fully that the judgment seat of Christ will issue in chastisement for unworthy living by Christians, but this will not be inflicted after resurrection.

(viii) Rev. 11:18 repays exact study. The four and twenty elders worship God because He has put forth His "power, His great power" (*teen dunamin sou teen megaleen*) and has exercised His sovereignty. In consequence of this asserting of power there are five results. (1) The nations are angry, (2) God's wrath replies, (3) there arrives "the season for the dead to be judged," (4) for the faithful to be rewarded, and (5) for the destruction of the destroyers of the earth.

Since prophets and saints are to receive their reward at the resurrection of the just (Luke 14:14), the first resurrection (Rev. 20:1-6), the season for the dead to be judged and rewarded is here found directly before the destruction of the Antichrist and his helpers in the wasting of the lands.

Concerning this judging of the dead three features are to be noted.

1. It must be of godly dead, for it is before the thousand years, whereas the judgment of the ungodly dead is thereafter (Rev. 20:1, 11-15).

2. It is a judgment of persons who are dead at the time they are judged. There is no ground for reading in that they have been

raised from the dead before the judgment takes place. They are styled "the dead." No one would think of styling living persons "the dead." The term employed (*nekros*) is nowhere used of persons who are not actually dead, physically or morally. Moreover, resurrection does not of itself assure life. That unique and glorious change to be the portion of such as share the first resurrection (1 Cor. 15) is their special privilege; it does not attach to all resurrection. Dead persons can be raised dead. In John 5:29 our Lord creates a clear contrast: "They that have done good shall come forth unto resurrection of *life;* and they that have done evil unto resurrection of *judgment.*" The Lord did not say that they shall come forth out of the tombs *alive*, but that they shall come forth *unto* resurrection of life or "*unto* resurrection of judgment" (*eis anastasin*). There seems no scripture, indeed, that at the moment they come forth they have even a body, other than that psychical counterpart before noticed and which persists in the death state.

Thus in Rev. 20:12 also it is as *dead* that they are judged: "I saw the *dead* standing before the throne ... and the *dead* were judged." It should therefore be supposed that those there present whose names are found in the book of life will thereupon be restored to *life*, that is, will be given an immortal body, even as the Lord said: "The Father raiseth the dead (*egeirei tous nekrous*) *and* makes them *live* (*zoopoiei*), thus also the Son makes to live whom He will" (*zoopoiei*, John 5:21). Here two operations are distinguished by the "*and* makes them live."

3. The verb *to be judged*, "the season of the dead to be judged," is the infinitive passive aorist (*kritheenai*). Being an aorist it has the force of a completed and final action. But this final judgment, which disposes of the case, may be the conclusion of a process of judgment. This is seen in another place where this aorist is twice used, Acts 25:9-10. Festus asked Paul whether he would be willing to go up from Caesarea to Jerusalem "there *to be judged* of these things before me" Paul answered that he already stood before Caesar's court "where I ought *to be judged*" (*kritheenai*). Both Festus and Paul meant that a final verdict should be reached and the case be determined; hence the aorist. But the history shows that Paul had been many times before the courts, twice before the Sanhedrin and several times

before Felix (Acts 23 and 24). Thus this passage in Rev. 11:18 does not forbid that believers may have been before judged by Christ, either in this life or after death, or both; what it states is that at the season indicated the decision of the Lord will be given, announcing, as we suggest, whether the person is of the "blessed and holy" who are accounted worthy of the impending resurrection from among the dead and of place and reward in the kingdom then about to be inaugurated.

This short discussion is no more than suggestive, directed to certain obscurities and perplexities found in our main theme, designed to provoke enquiry so as further to elucidate truth and dispel darkness. May the Lord in grace use it to this end.

7
Appendix to Page 26

On the meaning of the genitive "of Christ" (*tou Christou*) in 1 Cor. 15:23.

(This critical study is submitted with respect to those able to examine it.)

The force of this genitive may be studied in the following passages.

1. In Acts 16:33 it is said of the jailer at Philippi that "he was baptized, himself and all those *of him* (*hoi autou*)," that is, all those who happened to form his household circle at that particular midnight hour.

2. In the first chapter of the epistle that is before us (1 Cor. 1:12) the apostle reproves the believers on account of the contentions among them. "Now this I mean, that each one of you saith, I am of Paul; and I of Apollos; and I of Cephas; and I *of Christ* (*Christou*)." It cannot be supposed that these believers were attributing their redemption to Paul, Apollos, or Peter; so that the meaning is, "I am of Paul's circle; I of Apollos'; I of Peter's; I of Christ's circle." It was sectionalism, schism, denominationalism, sectarianism; although all alike were on the only foundation (ch. 3:10-11).

Family relationship alone did not make the jailer's relatives to be "of him" at that particular hour. It was those who were actually in his house at that time, which would include servants and slaves (if any). All believers were equally children of God, but some were "of Paul," others "of Peter," etc. Thus these two instances show that it is not relationship, natural or spiritual, but open membership in a known visible circle that is the idea in the term "of him."

3. Romans 14:4 reads "Who art thou that judgest the servant of another? (*oiketees*, household dependent; Lk. 16:13; Acts 10:7; 1 Pet. 2:18: all places). To his own lord he standeth or falleth." Verses 7, 8 add: "For none of us liveth to himself, and none dieth to himself. For

whether we live, we live unto the Lord; or whether we die, we die unto the Lord: whether we live therefore, or die, we are the Lord's" (we are *of the Lord, tou Kuriou esmen*. The German can express this, as the Greek, by case ending, "*wir sind des Herrn,*" Elberfeld version). "For to this end Christ died, and lived again, that He might be Lord of [might rule over] both dead and living" (Darby). Christ's lordship, His proprietorship of and authority over all, is indisputable: in the apostle's argument all are assumed to be owning it: "he that regardeth the day, regardeth it unto the Lord: and he that eateth, eateth unto the Lord" (ver. 6); but, as we shall see shortly, not all believers do in fact own that lordship, or do not own it continuously and to the end of life. Thus ideally all are "of Him," but actually some who might be, and ought to be, are not.[1]

4. This same meaning is to be seen in 2 Cor. 10:7, "Ye look at the things that are before your face. [It is something visible that is in question.] If anyone has confidence in himself *of Christ* to be (*Christou einai*), this let him consider with himself, that as he is *of Christ* (*Christou*) thus also are we": that is, I Paul am evidently and obviously of Christ's circle at least as much as my critic is: in proof of which he adduces the known public features of the measure and power of his ministry of the Word, which were the Lord's open acknowledgment of His faithful servant.

5. The same thought of a circle of persons that may be contrasted with other circles lies in the statement in Gal. 5:24, "And those *of Christ Jesus* (*hoi tou Christou Ieesou*) crucified the flesh with the [its] passions and the [its] cravings." In fallen human nature there works

---

1. Herodotus narrates that Astyages, king of the Medes, ordered a courtier, Harpagus, to kill the infant Cyrus, the king's grandson. The courtier says: "But for safety's sake it is necessary for me that this child should die; it is necessary however that *one of those of Astyages himself* (*tōn tina Astyageos*) should be the slayer and not (one) of mine (*tōn heemōn*). This he said and straightway sent a messenger to (one) of the herdsmen *of Astyages* (*tōn Astyageos*) whom he knew. . ." and left the matter to him (Hdt. I. 109, 110). Here two circles are distinguished, that of the king and that of the courtier, and each, in relation to its head, is described by the genitive. This force of the genitive occasions in English the italicized words in 1 Cor. 1:11, "them *which are of the household* of Chloe," where the original has simply *tōn Chloees* (those of Chloe).

a powerful principle of evil, described in christian terms as, "the old man which gets more and more corrupt according to the [its] deceitful cravings" (Eph. 4:22). Its cravings deceive man into indulging them, because they promise satisfaction though they produce corruption. Through partaking of the divine nature the believer in Christ is afforded a way of escaping "from the corruption that is in the world through lust [the cravings of the old man]" (2 Pet. 1:4); but it abides a certainty, to the Christian as well as to the unbeliever, "that the one sowing to the flesh out of the flesh shall reap corruption" (Gal. 6:8).

How this corrupting principle in human nature originated perplexed philosophers and how to master it baffled moralists. Various schools had different methods. The circle of Epicurus proposed the sensually agreeable plan of stifling the flesh by satiating it. That of the Stoics advocated a stern rigid suppression. Eastern philosophy, as in Buddhism, recommended a sustained passive ignoring of all desire.

The circle which bore the name of Christ Jesus had a method peculiar to itself. It was neither satiating, suppressing, nor ignoring, but *crucifying:* "those of Christ Jesus *crucified* the flesh." They taught that Christ died on account of the old man himself, as well as his corrupt doings. They held that, judicially, before God, man's creator and judge, the death of the Substitute was the death of the sinner, that therefore the old man "was crucified with Christ" (Rom. 6:6). The messengers of this faith offered a promise from God that whoever would accept from the heart this view, with its implications and practical consequences, should receive power from His eternal Spirit to live in freedom from the old tyranny of sin. The new method worked effectively where all other attempts had failed. Moral crucifixion with Christ led on to moral resurrection with Him, and the circle that bore His name became, as a circle, and by contrast, conspicuous for holiness.

No doubt this crucifixion was more distinctly apprehended and more fully exhibited by some than by others; we know that in fact some in the circle were not children of God at all—they seemed to be "*of* Christ Jesus" in the sense of publicly belonging to the circle that bore His name, though they were not *"in* Christ Jesus" by spiritual union: but the thought in the statement before us is that a certain known circle or school—"those of Christ Jesus"—was characterized by a certain attitude and doctrine, which its members were presumed to have adopted, and were expected and exhorted to maintain in practical conduct.

6. The important argument in Gal. 3:23-29 contains the same conception. "But if ye are *of Christ*, then are ye Abraham's seed, etc." (*ei de humeis Christou,* ver. 29). Those who fear God are viewed by Him in two classes: first, such as in spiritual growth are yet infants, and therefore under control by rules—"thou shalt . . . thou shalt not"; second, those who have become of age, grown up sons, who are freed from such restrictions, are at liberty. The former are under a tutor, the law (ver. 23-25), who orders their conduct, who restrains and punishes the outworking of their carnal nature: the "sons" are "of Christ" ("but if ye are of Christ"), Who enables them by the Spirit to walk by the free, holy impulses of the new nature.

Translation from the one status and association into the other is by faith and baptism: that is, by an act of the heart known to God, but also by a public act seen by men; for we become *"in* Christ Jesus by faith" (ver. 26), but we *"put on* Christ" by baptism (ver. 27). Thus here also to be "of Christ" means something more than to have exercised faith in Him, even to have associated openly by immersion with those who profess to have died out of the old circle and to have risen again into a new circle, that of Christ Jesus.

7. In 2 Tim. 2:19-21, the apostle again speaks of things plain and visible; such as a foundation stone, and the inscription carved upon it; a house built on the foundation; the various utensils of the house, of either valuable or common materials, gold and silver or wood and earth.

The picture is very like Paul's earlier metaphor in 1 Cor. 3, where also is the foundation, the superstructure, the precious or the perishable materials, either of which may be built by the believer into the life-work and character which each is erecting on the one foundation. He exhorts the Corinthian Christians not to use the perishable: in Timothy he exhorts to purge out of one's character the common elements, that the gold and silver of the divine nature, created in us by the Spirit upon the ground of redemption, may alone remain, and one be thus a vessel fit for the immediate use of the divine Master, not one relegated to the lower purposes of the great house.

The said inscription on the foundation reads thus: "Knows the Lord those being of Him (*tous ontas autou*), and, Let every one naming the name of the Lord depart from unrighteousness." That is, the Lord, on His side, knows distinctly each one who in reality, according to the Lord's standard, is of His circle. On our side the sign that warrants any person being accorded by us a place in that circle is that he forsakes unrighteousness. He who never yet has forsaken unrighteousness (wrong doing, *adikia*, as 1 Cor. 6:8-9) is not "of Him," (that is, not as the Lord judges), even though he may hold membership in a Christian church. He who having forsaken wrongdoing afterward returns thereto is to be put out of the Christian circle (1 Cor. 5:13), and thus ceases to be "of Him" for the purposes of this expression.

This does not affect the final salvation of every believer; for one is saved before he is added to the church, and therefore final salvation does not depend upon membership in that privileged company who will form "the church." This cuts away the root of the Romish error that one must belong to the church to be saved. But the wrong doers of the church circle are plainly warned that they "shall not inherit God's kingdom" (1 Cor. 6:9: etc.). Such will not be "accounted worthy of the kingdom of God" (2 Thess. 1:5, 11), and hence will not be of the "blessed and holy" who will rise in that first resurrection which assures reigning in that kingdom.

8. The expression under review is in Romans 8:9: "But ye are not in flesh but in spirit, if at least spirit of God dwells in you. But if any one has not spirit of Christ, this one is not of Him."

The omission from verse 1 preceding of the clause "who walk not according to flesh but according to spirit" is of first importance, showing that the justification of a believer in Christ is not dependent upon his walk as a Christian. At the very moment that a repenting sinner rests his salvation upon the atoning work that Christ accomplished upon the cross, and therefore before he has had opportunity for doing any works, he acquires a new standing. By that faith in Christ he obtains access to the standing of one who is in the favour of God (Rom. 5:1, 2). He is then and there seen by God, his judge, no longer as he is in himself, but as he now is "in Christ." He is deemed to have met his doom and to be free therefrom. The storm of wrath due to him on account of his sins has burst upon him in the person of his Divine Substitute: he has thus endured its full fury; that storm has exhausted itself, and "there is therefore now no condemnation to them that are in Christ Jesus."

But this eternally justified believer may henceforth walk either by the impulses of his old fleshly nature or by the leading of that new spirit nature which is created in us when we believe on Christ. That a justified person may walk "according to flesh" is certain from many Scriptures and much sad experience. "I, brethren," says Paul, "was not able [formerly] to speak to you as to spiritual but as fleshly . . . But neither yet now am I able, for yet fleshly ye are. For whereas there is among you jealousy and strife, are ye not fleshly, and walk according to men," that is, not according to God? (1 Cor. 3:1-3. See also Gal. 5:13-26, for a sustained contrast between "flesh" and "spirit," the old nature and the new, in the believer).

To the Romans the apostle declared that if they lived according to flesh they would be unable to please God and were liable to die (8:7, 8, and comp. 1 Cor. 10:1-6). Upon this possibility of premature death we have before spoken. But, he adds, "ye are not in flesh but in spirit, if at least (*eiper*) spirit of God dwells in you." This "if at least"[2] shows clearly the possibility of one who is for ever free from condemnation not being indwelt by "spirit of God." It is God the Spirit Who creates and energises the new nature, but it is not the Holy Spirit as a person that is here in view: the question is whether the believer is ruled still by the mind of the old nature, which is "flesh," or by the mind of the new nature, which is "spirit," according to the exhortations "be renewed in the spirit of your mind": "Have this mind in you which was also in Christ Jesus" (Eph. 4:23: Phil.

---

2. "The Greek particle is more than merely 'if' (which often equals 'since' or 'as'), and suggests just such *doubt* and *enquiry* as would amount to self-examination. See 2 Cor. 13:5." Moule, Camb. Bible for Schools, *in loco*. So Alford: "if so be that ('provided that'; not 'since' . . . that this is the meaning here is evident by the exception which immediately follows)."

2:5). And, adds the Scripture (Rom. 8:9), "If any one has not spirit of Christ, this one (emphatic) is not *of Him* (*ouk estin autou*)."

In the light of the other places considered this will mean that one not ruled by the same spirit which animated Christ is not of that company which He owns as His circle, His household. "He is not His (belongs not to Him, in the higher and blessed sense of being united to Him as a *member* of Him)" Alford, *in loco;* italics mine.

In his learned critical work *Licht vom Osten* (*Light from the East*—ed. iv. 322) Professor Adolph Deissmann has remarked upon the parallel between this genitive *Christou,* of Christ, and *doulos Christou* Christ's slave, and the expressions *Kaisaros* of Caesar, and *Caesar's slave,* belonging to Caesar, his own personal property; that is, his personal retinue and slaves as distinct from the vast host of his subjects outside of his immediate household. In illustration he cites several of the passages here examined, including the one chiefly before us, 1 Cor. 15:22, "they that are *of Christ* in His Parousia." This usage is found in Phil. 4:22: "All the saints salute you, especially they that are of Caesar's household" (*hoi ek tees Kaisaros oikias*). Comp. also Matt. 22:21 and parallels: "the things that are Caesar's" (of Caesar, *ta Kaisaros*) contrasted with the other circle, "the things that are God's" (*ta tou Theou*). Similarly, Christ also has a vast number who do acknowledge Him as Saviour but have not learned to be His *slaves,* and so are not "of Him" within the force of this term.

Also from Kingsley Press
AN ORDERED LIFE
AN AUTOBIOGRAPHY BY G. H. LANG

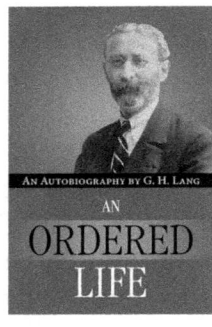

G. H. Lang was a remarkable Bible teacher, preacher and writer of a past generation who should not be forgotten by today's Christians. He inherited the spiritual "mantle" of such giants in the faith as George Müller, Anthony Norris Groves and other notable saints among the early Brethren movement. He traveled all over the world with no fixed means of support other than prayer and faith and no church or other organization to depend on. Like Mr. Müller before him, he told his needs to no one but God. Many times his faith was tried to the limit, as funds for the next part of his journey arrived only at the last minute and from unexpected sources.

This autobiography traces in precise detail the dealings of God with his soul, from the day of his conversion at the tender age of seven, through the twilight years when bodily infirmity restricted most of his former activities. You will be amazed, as you read these pages, to see how quickly and continually a soul can grow in grace and in the knowledge of spiritual things if they will wholly follow the Lord.

Horace Bushnell once wrote that every man's life is a plan of God, and that it's our duty as human beings to find and follow that plan. As Mr. Lang looks back over his long and varied life in the pages of this book, he frequently points out the many times God prepared him in the present for some future work or role. Spiritual life applications abound throughout the book, making it not just a life story but a spiritual training manual of sorts. Preachers will find sermon starters and illustrations in every chapter. Readers of all kinds will benefit from this close-up view of the dealings of God with the soul of one who made it his life's business to follow the Lamb wherever He should lead.

Buy online at our website: **www.KingsleyPress.com**
Also available as an eBook for Kindle, Nook and iBooks.

ANTHONY NORRIS GROVES
SAINT AND PIONEER
by G. H. Lang

Although his name is little known in Christian cirlces today, Anthony Norris Groves (1795-1853) was, according to the writer of this book, one of the most influential men of the nineteenth century. He was what might be termed a spiritual pioneer, forging a path through unfamiliar territory in order that others might follow. One of those who followed him was George Müller, known to the world as one who in his lifetime cared for over ten thousand orphans without any appeal for human aid, instead trusting God alone to provide for the daily needs of this large enterprise.

In 1825 Groves wrote a booklet called *Christian Devotedness* in which he encouraged fellow believers and especially Christian workers to take literally Jesus' command not to lay up treasures on earth, but rather to give away their savings and possessions toward the spread of the gospel and to embark on a life of faith in God alone for the necessaries of life. Groves himself took this step of faith: he gave away his fortune, left his lucrative dental practice in England, and went to Baghdad to establish the first Protestant mission to Arabic-speaking Muslims. His going was not in connection with any church denomination or missionary society, as he sought to rely on God alone for needed finances. He later went to India also.

His approach to missions was to simplify the task of churches and missions by returning to the methods of Christ and His apostles, and to help indigenous converts form their own churches without dependence on foreign support. His ideas were considered radical at the time but later became widely accepted in evangelical circles.

Groves was a leading figure in the early days of what Robert Govett would later call the mightiest movement of the Spirit of God since Pentecost—a movement that became known simply as the Brethren. In this book G. H. Lang combines a study of the life and influence of Anthony Norris Groves with a survey of the original principles and practices of the Brethren movement.

The Churches of God
by G. H. Lang

If you've ever wondered what the churches of the New Testament looked like—how they functioned, how they were governed, how they conducted their evangelistic and missionary enterprises, what ordinances they observed, what their liturgy consisted of, how decisions were made, how discipline was administered; if you've ever wondered how far modern churches have drifted from the New Testament pattern; if you've ever wondered what it would take for your church, and others like it, to return to the New Testament model, or if such a thing is even possible or desirable—then this book is for you!

G. H. Lang's ability to elucidate Biblical truth was never more evident than in this small treatise on the constitution, government, discipline and ministry of the church of God. His gifts as a diligent Bible student, expositor, and precise thinker, together with his many years of experience as an itinerant Bible teacher in many different countries and cultural settings, all combine to make this a go-to reference on many issues relating to the local church.

About the Author

G. H. Lang (1874-1958) was a gifted Bible teacher and prolific author who in his early life was associated with the "exclusive" branch of the Plymouth Brethren but later affiliated himself with the Open Brethren. He traveled widely as an itinerant Bible teacher, depending solely on God for his support. Although Mr. Lang himself was a prolific author, it was his belief that "no man should write a book until he is 40. He needs to prove his theories in practice before publishing." In his own case, all but nine of his many books were written after he was 50. Kingsley Press has recently re-published Lang's amazing autobiography, *An Ordered Life*. More information can be found on our web site: www.KingsleyPress.com.

Lord, Teach Us to Pray
By Alexander Whyte

Dr. Alexander Whyte (1836-1921) was widely acknowledged to be the greatest Scottish preacher of his day. He was a mighty pulpit orator who thundered against sin, awakening the consciences of his hearers, and then gently leading them to the Savior. He was also a great teacher, who would teach a class of around 500 young men after Sunday night service, instructing them in the way of the Lord more perfectly.

In the later part of Dr. Whyte's ministry, one of his pet topics was prayer. Luke 11:1 was a favorite text and was often used in conjunction with another text as the basis for his sermons on this subject. The sermons printed here represent only a few of the many delivered. But each one is deeply instructive, powerful and convicting.

Nobody else could have preached these sermons; after much reading and re-reading of them that remains the most vivid impression. There can be few more strongly personal documents in the whole literature of the pulpit. . . . When all is said, there is something here that defies analysis—something titanic, something colossal, which makes ordinary preaching seem to lie a long way below such heights as gave the vision in these words, such forces as shaped their appeal. We are driven back on the mystery of a great soul, dealt with in God's secret ways and given more than the ordinary measure of endowment and grace. His hearers have often wondered at his sustained intensity; as Dr. Joseph Parker once wrote of him: "many would have announced the chaining of Satan for a thousand years with less expenditure of vital force" than Dr. Whyte gave to the mere announcing of a hymn. —*From the Preface*

Buy online at our website: **www.KingsleyPress.com**
Also available as an eBook for Kindle, Nook and iBooks.

The Awakening
By Marie Monsen

REVIVAL! It was a long time coming. For twenty long years Marie Monsen prayed for revival in China. She had heard reports of how God's Spirit was being poured out in abundance in other countries, particularly in nearby Korea; so she began praying for funds to be able to travel there in order to bring back some of the glowing coals to her own mission field. But that was not God's way. The still, small voice of God seemed to whisper, "What is happening in Korea can happen in China if you will pay the price in prayer." Marie Monsen took up the challenge and gave her solemn promise: "Then I will pray until I receive."

The Awakening is Miss Monsen's own vivid account of the revival that came in answer to prayer. Leslie Lyall calls her the "pioneer" of the revival movement—the handmaiden upon whom the Spirit was first poured out. He writes: "Her surgical skill in exposing the sins hidden within the Church and lurking behind the smiling exterior of many a trusted Christian—even many a trusted Christian leader—and her quiet insistence on a clear-cut experience of the new birth set the pattern for others to follow."

The emphasis in these pages is on the place given to prayer both before and during the revival, as well as on the necessity of self-emptying, confession, and repentance in order to make way for the infilling of the Spirit.

One of the best ways to stir ourselves up to pray for revival in our own generation is to read the accounts of past awakenings, such as those found in the pages of this book. Surely God is looking for those in every generation who will solemnly take up the challenge and say, with Marie Monsen, "I will pray until I receive."

Buy online at our website: **www.KingsleyPress.com**
Also available as an eBook for Kindle, Nook and iBooks.

A Present Help
By Marie Monsen

Does your faith in the God of the impossible need reviving? Do you think that stories of walls of fire and hosts of guardian angels protecting God's children are only for Bible times? Then you should read the amazing accounts in this book of how God and His unseen armies protected and guided Marie Monsen, a Norwegian missionary to China, as she traveled through bandit-ridden territory spreading the Gospel of Jesus Christ and standing on the promises of God. You will be amazed as she tells of an invading army of looters who ravaged a whole city, yet were not allowed to come near her mission compound because of angels standing sentry over it. Your heart will thrill as she tells of being held captive on a ship for twenty-three days by pirates whom God did not allow to harm her, but instead were compelled to listen to her message of a loving Savior who died for their sin. As you read the many stories in this small volume your faith will be strengthened by the realization that our God is a living God who can still bring protection and peace in the midst of the storms of distress, confusion and terror—a very present help in trouble.

Buy online at our website: **www.KingsleyPress.com**
Also available as an eBook for Kindle, Nook and iBooks.

GOD'S FIRST WORDS

Studies in Genesis
Historic, Prophetic and Experimental

This overview of the first book of the Bible shows that the first words contained in Genesis are enlarged and unfolded in a great many different directions and applications throughout the rest of the Bible, but the words themselves are never changed and they are never any more perfect in the last book in the Bible than they are in the first.

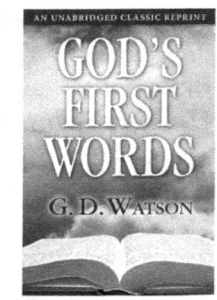

"In the beginning God" (Genesis 1:1). No other book in the universe could ever begin like this except it were the book of God. These first words in the Bible prove that the book has a divine author; that it is not an invention of the human mind, for the very first expression is of such a character as to put it beyond all the thinking of the natural mind. There is no attempt to prove the existence of God, there is no prelude, but out from the vast eternity comes the simple, sublime expression that God was at the beginning.

G. D. Watson (1845-1924) has been called an "apostle to the sanctified." He was a holiness preacher and evangelist whose ministry took him to England, the West Indies, New Zealand, Australia, Japan and Korea. He authored a number of books on the sanctified life, including *Our Own God, Soul Food, A Pot of Oil, Pure Gold, White Robes, God's Eagles* and several more.

Buy online at our website: **www.KingsleyPress.com**
This book is also available as an eBook for Kindle, Nook and iBooks.